STOP PROCRASTINATING

BREAKING THE PROCRASTINATION HABIT. A
SIMPLE GUIDE TO HACKING LAZINESS AND
BUILDING SELF DISCIPLINE

MARK BOURNE

DISCLAIMER

This book is not intended as a substitute for the medical advice of physicians. The reader should regularly consult a physician in matters relating to his/her health and particularly with respect to any symptoms that may require diagnosis or medical attention.

No part of this book may be reproduced or transmitted in any form or by any means, electronic or mechanical, including photocopying, recording or by any information storage and retrieval system, without written permission from the author.

The information provided within this book is for general informational purposes only. While we try to keep the information up-to-date and correct, there are no representations or warranties, express or implied, about the completeness, accuracy, reliability, suitability or availability concerning the information, products, services, or related graphics contained in this book for any purpose. Any use of this information is at your own risk.

The methods described in this book are the author's thoughts. They are not intended to be a definitive set of instructions for this project. You may discover there are other methods and materials to accomplish the same result.

CONTENTS

INTRODUCTION

What is Procrastination?

A procrastinating attitude can be defined as one in which the individual chooses to do a less important task rather than a more important one. The reasons for this procrastinating attitude could be many and another chapter in this book discusses them in detail. The most important result of procrastinating is the piling up of important tasks to such an extent that doing them could actually prove to be counterproductive later on.

For an individual to be called a procrastinator, he or she must consistently indulge in doing less urgent and needless tasks over more urgent and important tasks in such a way that these needless unimportant tasks become counterproductive in the life of the individual.

Many people know, realize and experience the negative

and sometimes, *q*uite devastating, effects of procrastinating both in their personal and professional lives. Some of these people feel a sense of guilt and they are overcome by an overwhelming sense of loss of productivity, which can motivate these people in the short-term. However, soon they are back to their erring ways especially when they achieve success with one or two tasks and/or can give themselves seemingly irrefutable reasons for the acts of procrastination.

For people who are keen on permanently eliminating the procrastinating attitude, a little more hard work, determination and dedication are needed than merely depending on an occasional sense of guilt about the negative attitude. People who are intent on overcoming this challenge must rise above the basic instincts of wanting to find reasons and excuses for their attitude and, instead, take up cudgels against it in a serious and consistent way.

Here are some common ways that people use to procrastinate. When you identify and recognize these traits you will be in a better position to manage them:

Avoiding – You deliberately avoid the situation or location when or where the task needs to be done. For example, you deliberately miss appointments or avoid going to the office thinking that you can use this excuse for not doing the job.

Distraction – You intentionally immerse yourself in or engage in another activity to enable you to forget about the important task that needs your attention

Trivialize the issue – You try to tell yourself that the work you are putting off is not as important as it seems. You try to trivialize the importance of the task at hand.

Comparing with others seemingly worse off – You try to compare your situation with someone else's, which you believe is worse than your situation and use this excuse to forgive yourself for the procrastinating attitude.

Making it sound funny – You tend to use humor to present your lack of productivity and achievement in such a way that people find the situation funny and laugh at it giving you a sense of freedom from the guilt. However, remember the only person losing out because of this needless humor is you.

Blaming an external element – You intentionally find fault with external factors beyond your control such as people not appreciating your earlier work or someone didn't complete his part and so you cannot do your part etc. You use these external factors as an excuse for your procrastinating attitude.

Denying the procrastinating attitude – You tell yourself that you are not procrastinating at all and the work you are doing right now is more important than the one you are putting off for later.

Laziness Vs Procrastination

While it is common for people to use laziness as one of the reasons for procrastinating, there are some fundamental differences between the two. Recognizing and identifying these differences in your attitude will help you clearly discern between the two so that you can manage and handle them differently.

A lazy person is one who does not like to make any extra effort at all. The individual will remain idle instead of doing anything or do something where the effort required to do the task is minimal. The motivation for laziness comes from the huge difference that exists between having to put in the effort and having to do the right thing. In fact, indolence which is a synonym for laziness comes from a Latin term, 'indolentia,' which translates to 'without taking trouble' or 'without effort.' Idleness is associated with laziness.

A procrastinator, on the other hand, will rarely remain idle while he or she postpones the important tasks. These individuals will do something that they like to do or find pleasure in and do not remain idle. Remember, postponing a task for a useful purpose is not procrastination.

Postponing a task must necessarily make the situation worse than it is for it to be deemed procrastination.

Let me illustrate with an example. It is perfectly in order for you to put off filing your tax returns until you receive all the required data from all financial sources. However, it is procrastination if you do not file your returns because you want to go on a holiday and the result of not filing the return is a hefty fine.

Laziness necessarily involves lack of effort or remaining idle whereas procrastination is putting off important tasks while choosing to do some pleasurable task. A lazy person may never complete the task at hand whereas a procrastinator will definitely complete it at some point in time *q*uite possibly at a higher cost to himself or herself.

Procrastination comes more from a sense of boredom because the work, though extremely necessary, is boring or uninteresting. A procrastinating attitude is a result of the inability to control and check impulsive behavior and prevent yourself from giving into small and short-term emotional pleasures of doing something that you like over doing something that is critical at that point in time.

There are many reasons that drive people to procrastinate. This book aims to give you some insights on these reasons, some unavoidable effects of procrastinating, along with one particularly easy-to-follow trick to overthrow procrastination from your life. This technique, aptly called the 3...2...1 trick, is essentially very straightforward and easy to follow. However, the challenge is being consistent and determined in your efforts to implement it until it becomes a habit.

I have chosen to dedicate one particular chapter to time management because this skill is the core of any approach to discipline, which is essentially what we are trying to do while attempting to ruthlessly root out procrastination from our lives. In addition to the 3...2...1 trick, I have also included some general tips on helping you overcome this debilitating habit of putting off important tasks unnecessarily.

CHAPTER 1: WHY DO WE LOVE TO PROCRASTINATE?

The key element in trying to find a solution to any problem is to first try and understand the problem from all angles. This and the next chapters are dedicated to the reasons for people to procrastinate and the effects of procrastination. When you can understand the why of a problem, the how to overcome answer will become clearer and easier to follow than otherwise.

Additionally, when you become aware of the negative aspects of doing something wrong, your mind will be more prone to accept lessons to overcome these negative effects. That is the reason to definitely include the negative effects of procrastination in the next chapter.

Why do we love to put off important tasks?

While you will find plenty of reasons as to why you enjoy

putting off doing important tasks, most of the reasons would usually fit into one or more of the following four primary reasons for procrastination. So, here goes:

A deep fear of failure – Every one of us hates to fail. Some of us are better equipped to handle failure than others. Yet, the fear of failure always lingers long and large over our heads. People use procrastination as a method to manage this fear of failure. It is more comforting to know that you did not do the job rather than you did the job and failed.

Procrastination becomes a shield or a protecting mechanism against the deep-seated fear of failure. Many people prefer to manage the subjective fear of not even attempting the task rather than the actual and objective fear of attempting and failing at the job. Handling fear of failure is not easy, but running away from this fear is not a solution at all.

Ask yourself the question, why are you putting off the task? And believe me, this could be one of the reasons on many occasions when you have procrastinated.

A lack of purpose or focus – People who procrastinate are those that lack a sense of focus or purpose in their lives. They are not sure of the way their life is going or are uncertain of how to take control of what is happening in their lives. If you do not have a purpose or a target you want to work towards (both in the short-term and in the long-term), you are bound to be a procrastinator.

If you do not know or cannot identify the end point, you will end up using energy reserves unnecessarily on things that may not add any value to your life. A powerful goal and a robust strategy to move towards the goal are key ingredients to help you keep your focus and help you overcome the challenge of procrastination.

Low Energy Levels – Insufficient mental and/or physical strength is a key contributor for a procrastinating attitude. It is imperative that you lead a healthy lifestyle with sufficient intake of nutritious food, a healthy dose of sleep and an active lifestyle to keep a healthy body and mind. If you are feeling fatigued most of the time, how can you do the work that is needed?

Another problem associated with low energy levels is that you could be suffering from depression or anxiety issues. If you find yourself getting needlessly restless, then it would do you good to get yourself checked by a medical professional.

The problem of low energy level is very easy to identify. If you want to do more but find it difficult to do more, then you are a victim of low energy levels. Work on your lifestyle habits and get into action. Then, this excuse will not be a common problem for you.

An obsession with perfection – This is another extremely common problem that a procrastinator faces. An individual is so obsessed with perfection that he or she does not want to start off the task unless the person is thoroughly well-versed with all the elements needed to do the job resulting in procrastinating.

The obsession with perfection could affect your

confidence levels about a particular job especially if it is new and you are still in the learning curve. You fear that you may not obtain a result to your satisfaction and this obsession with perfection will make you want to put off the task until you feel more confident and are sure about achieving the end result that will make you happy.

While wanting to be perfect is a great personality trait to have, if it reaches an obsessive level, then you need to rein it in. If the call for perfection is preventing you from even starting off, then it is not a great sign. It is better to be less than perfect but complete your task when you need to complete it. Beware of this 'perfect' obsession. It could obstruct your pathway to success more than you would like.

Wanting to be perfect at all times means you have no compassion for yourself. If you don't tell yourself that you are human and perfection cannot be achieved at all times, you will find the energy and the wherewithal to take up and complete important tasks.

Types of procrastinators

There are different types of procrastinators depending on why they put off tasks for later or until the last minute. Here is a brief description of each of them. Find out which one you belong to and then you will find it easier to overcome the problems.

Procrastinators who enjoy a thrill – There are many thrill-seekers in this world who deliberately put off doing a task until the last minute because they believe that they thrive under excessive pressure and stress. Yes, there are people who claim to love the adrenaline rush when they are compelled to nearly push themselves over the edge to complete the task at the very last minute. The *q*uestion to ask such people is this: are they able to fully use their potential and do the task to the best of their abilities to get optimum results?

Procrastinators who love to avoid things – The person who avoids getting out of his or her comfort zone is an avoiding procrastinator. Avoiding procrastinators are *q*uite worried about what others will think of them. They run away because they are scared of failure and sometimes, scared of handling the after-effects of success too. They prefer people to think of them as being lazy rather than as not having the ability to do something.

Procrastinators who cannot decide – These are the people who simply cannot decide one way or the other. These procrastinators are usually very fearful of any negative outcomes that can happen because of their decision. These people are normally people who hate responsibilities of all kinds and run away from them. They believe that if they didn't make the choice then the bad result is not their fault.

Procrastinators who are obsessed with perfection – These are the people who set such high standards for themselves that they cannot but feel overwhelmed by their own expectations. These people may not have a problem starting off on their tasks. But, they will find it difficult to complete the task on or before time because of the unrealistic expectations they have from themselves. Their obsessive drive for perfection ensures that they end up doing nothing at all.

Procrastinators who are always busy – There are some people who are so busy at all times that they do not find the time to actually sit down and prioritize their tasks. For such procrastinators, all the tasks appear equally important and hence they are unable to discern between the really important ones and the seemingly important ones resulting in critical tasks not getting done at the appropriate time.

So, now that you know the reasons behind why people procrastinate and also the types of procrastinators, it will be easy to identify which category you belong to and then focus on those tips that help that particular category in an optimum way.

CHAPTER 2: NEGATIVE EFFECTS OF PROCRASTINATION

Knowing about the negative effects of an attitude can be a great motivating factor to work hard to overcome the attitude. Hence, I have chosen to dedicate this chapter to what and how things can go wrong if you allow your procrastinating attitude to take over your life.

You are bound to lose precious time

Time is of the essence in this fast-paced world. Moreover, time is the only commodity that can never be replaced. One dollar lost can be earned again through hard work whereas one second lost is lost forever. You simply cannot turn back the hands of time and there will be nothing left except regret if you keep procrastinating and not getting down to work.

There are few feelings which are worse than knowing for a fact that if only if you had had the good sense to take that first step instead of putting it off. Do not allow this unpleasant situation in your life to happen. Take that first step and you will see how easy it is to take the next steps.

You will miss out on great opportunities

How many times in life have you turned back and said, "Oh, I wish I had taken that opportunity when I had it instead of leaving it because I feared failure!" More often than not, opportunities happen only once and rarely do people get a second chance. Do not allow your procrastinating attitude make you lose out on taking advantage of some great opportunities. Opportunities are nature's way of telling you that you are capable of being successful and that is why they came and knocked at your door. Please don't put off answering the door.

You are bound to miss out on your goals

When you procrastinate, you are putting off achieving your goals as well. If you cannot take that first step, you are bound to miss out on these goals that you have set for yourself. It might seem strange to you that your mind is not allowing you to do something that you deeply desire. What you need to know in such situations is to dig deeper and rid your mind of all layers of resistance and you will find willpower and strength lurking there in the depths of your psyche.

When you set goals and give in to procrastination, you are like that frog who is trying to jump out of the well. He jumps one step forward and falls back two steps. That is what will happen to you and your goals too. Procrastinating will lead you away from your own goals and desires instead of towards them.

Your career will be affected negatively

One of the first places the negative effects of procrastination will be reflected in is your workplace. This attitude will ruin your chances for promotions as you may not be meeting deadlines at the right time and with the right *q*uality of work. You are highly likely to miss out on monthly deadlines and targets because of your putting off attitude and this will sooner than later reflect in the way your career is moving. Missing targets and goals are not good for your career at all.

You will end up making poor decisions and choices

When you procrastinate, you are pushing things to the last minute when there is a huge amount of stress and pressure on you because there is very little time left to complete the work. These high levels of stress can compel you to take decisions and make choices that may not be optimal for the task at hand.

Moreover, under such pressures, you become emotionally weak too and this will influence bad decisions even more. If you had not procrastinated, the chances that your decisions are sound and based on objective thinking are much higher than if you procrastinate. Wrong decisions can have a long-term effect on the *q*uality of your life.

You will have lower self-esteem

It is *q*uite strange that one of the reasons for a procrastinating attitude is a lack of self-confidence and when you use that as an excuse and not do your work then your self-esteem will dip lower than before. You started off doubting your capabilities and hence not doing what you have to do. But, when you do not complete tasks, you will feel unhappy with yourself and your self- confidence will be dented further.

You will continue to ask *q*uestions such as, "Why can't I simply start the work?" and getting no satisfactory answer for this, you will feel worse than ever. So, low self-esteem is both a cause and an effect of procrastination.

Your personal and professional reputation will take a hit

If you keep making promises and fail to live up to them then your reputation is bound to take a big hit. Nobody will believe your words anymore. At the personal front, people will begin to doubt your intentions and stay away from you. At the professional front, your bosses and colleagues will never take your word for it and will keep checking on your progress enhancing your level of pressure and nervousness. Loss of professional reputation can even end up in loss of jobs!

Your health will be affected badly

Procrastination is directly connected to stress and anxiety which are, in turn, connected to your physical, emotional, and mental health. As you continue to procrastinate, you will become depressed because either you are not working at all or your last-minute efforts at doing tasks are resulting in unsatisfactory outcomes. These anxieties, stresses, and depressions will ultimately take its toll on your overall health.

Moreover, if you are a procrastinator then you must be putting off important tasks such as exercising, visits to the doctor, and other activities that are directly related to your health. Hence, procrastination without control will definitely affect your mental and physical health negatively. Now that you are aware of the negative effects of procrastination, let us dive straight into the easy 3...2...1 trick so that you can get a hold of your life and make it more positive and energetic than now.

CHAPTER 3: THE 3...2...1 TRICK

Now that you know what procrastination is, and how badly it can affect your life, it makes sense to find the wherewithal to beat this monster. Let me give you this extremely simple 3...2...1 trick that worked wonders for me.

Procrastination was like a rotten core eating away into my life. People were so focused on my procrastinating attitude that my skills and talents simply blended into the background and I became an average worker at work and an average friend, son, or anyone else in a personal relationship. I knew deep down that I was definitely way above average and this debilitating attitude of procrastination was making me come across to people as average.

I needed to take control of my life and I wanted something that I could start with easily. I wanted a simple and uncomplicated solution that will rid me of this menace.

And, believe me, when I tell you that the 3...2...1 trick worked like magic. Here is how it works.

Look at one task that you have been putting off for a while now. Let me take something extremely basic like clearing the dustbin in your room. You need to lift up the bin, take it out of your room, and dump the contents in the larger dustbin kept outside your house to be picked up by the garbage truck on its next visit. For reasons already mentioned in this book, you have chosen not to do this deed.

Now, look at the dustbin in your room and count backward 3...2...1 and when you reach the 1, get up, lift the bin, and dump the contents wherever. Simple! Well, the trick is when you reach the 1, stop everything you are doing, get up and clear your dustbin. Initially, the only rules that you need to consider when you choose to take up a task using this 3...2...1 trick are:

The task must be doable and possible to do

The task can be done right at the time you are thinking about doing it

For example, you cannot have a task like traveling to Alaska from New York for this trick to work. That requires planning and yes, you can use this trick provided you break down the Alaska trip into small doable tasks and do each one of them by counting 3...2...1! But, for now, take tasks that are immediately doable.

Let us look at the trash bin example again. Now, it is a

different scenario. You are back home after a hard day's work and you are still working on some office emails. You walk into the room and see the trash bin full and you tell yourself, "I need to get the trash out. But, wait. Let me finish the emails and then I will do it."

This is the point where you stop, put your phone or any other device down, count 3...2...1 and when you reach 1, reach out for the bin and take it out! If you notice, you were resorting to procrastination when you said to yourself that you will take it out after finishing the emails. The emails can wait 2 minutes, can they not?

Let us look at another example for this trick. When the alarm rings in the morning, you snooze it about four times before you wake up, right? For the first day, don't wait for the fourth time.

After you hit it for the third time, count 3...2...1 and get off your bed. Do this for a couple of days.

Then, try to eliminate the third time as well. After you have hit the snooze button for the second time, count 3...2...1 and get off from your bed. After a couple of days, move it to the first time. The alarm rings, you count 3...2...1, get off from the bed, and switch off the alarm.

This worked like magic for me. Yes, it didn't happen easily. But, when I put my mind to it, I did it and my snooze button is permanently off!

Make it a habit

The trick in this 3...2...1 trick is to make it a habit. Don't do it for a day or two and forget about it afterward. Convert it into a habit. Thanks to Stephen Covey and his book, 7 Habits of Highly Effective People, it is now commonly accepted that if you do an activity for 21 days, then that activity becomes a habit deeply ingrained into your psyche. Well, for me converting the 3...2...1 trick into a habit did not need more than 2 weeks of concerted effort.

Every annoying task I was putting off, I consciously and deliberately used this trick and within 2 weeks, I was unconsciously counting 3...2...1 for every job I had to do. Don't hesitate to use it in all your to-be-done tasks such as cleaning dishes, feeding the dog, mowing the lawn, washing your clothes, reading that article that will help you make a great presentation at work, and anything else you can think of.

The thing about repeating the 3...2...1 trick is that you will find that each time you use, your are finding it easier to overcome the resistance your mind and body are putting up to prevent you from getting to the task. As the resistance keeps getting weaker, you will find motivation to do more and you would have found the value in the power of this seemingly deceptive trick.

This trick does more than helping you put out the trash or wash the dishes or doing other chores. Yes, these are also important. But, the true potential of this trick is to let you know the power of a positive habit and how you can start building such great habits with positive effects on your life by beginning with something very simple.

Once you have made it a habit, you can extend the 3...2...1 trick to more complex activities. For example, you know the importance of going for a walk every morning. You have already used the 3...2...1 trick to get up at the first alarm. Now, use the same 3...2...1 trick to get out from your house and go for the brisk walk or run! Alternately, you want to hit the gym. Say 3...2...1, sign up for a gym membership online and say 3...2...1 and leave for your first session.

The critical element in the 3...2...1 trick is that it must become so deeply ingrained into your psyche and when you start saying it, you are already reaching out to do the task, whatever it may be.

The same trick can be used for eliminating negative habits too. For example, you love pastries and you are trying your best not to eat one. You are looking at one of the most delicious cakes and you are dying to get in and buy it for yourself. You count 3...2...1 and when you reach 1, walk away from that place!

Similarly, if you wish to *q*uit smoking, you can use this trick. But, for this to work, the 3...2...1 trick must be powerfully ingrained in your brain. While your mind counts, your body must walk away from the bad habit. Use it every time you feel the urge to pick up a smoke. Say 3...2...1 and walk away. Do it until you *q*uit your habit of smoking.

The 3...2...1 trick may come across as a rather childish method initially. It might seem to you that it is like telling a little kid to do something *q*uickly before you finish counting to 5 or to 10, isn't it? But, this is such an effective techni*q*ue that allows you to start using it for the most basic task and then build it into more complex ones as well.

However, the important thing is to start immediately. You must find the courage and willpower to take that first step and keeping taking the next steps without faltering. Even if you falter, there is no problem, start again. Faltering and mistakes are all mere obstacles in the path of success.

Do not allow these temporary obstacles and setbacks to swerve you from the right path. So, 3...2...1, go!

CHAPTER 4: TIME MANAGEMENT

Time management skill is an essential aspect of keeping your procrastination attitude under check. Everyone has only 24 hours in a day. While some can manage to get a lot done in this time, there are others who manage to get very little done. The best achievers of the world are great time managers.

When you manage time well, you will be able to handle all tasks in the order of priority giving you lower chances of putting off important jobs that need your attention. Good time management will help you do your tasks in a calm and peaceful atmosphere without the frenzy of purposeless multitasking. Yes, sometimes multitasking is good to save time. But, it has to be included in the time management techniques to ensure that combining more than one task adds value to your entire day's functioning instead of merely appearing busy without much productive output.

So, it makes sense to understand what time management is and how to manage your time efficiently to avoid the negative effects of procrastination.

What is time management?

Time management is the process by which you organize and plan the available time each day to accomplish all tasks of that day. It is the skill that helps you allocate time to each and every activity of yours sufficiently so that it can be completely well and to your satisfaction. Time management skills enable you to work smarter in such a way that you do not end up wasting an unnecessarily large amount of time on a small task or leave very little time for a task that is considerably more difficult to do.

The benefits of time management are numerous and some of them are:

Improved efficiency and productivity leading to personal and professional growth Reduced procrastination by ensuring the completion of set tasks on time every time An improved professional and personal reputation

Less anxiety and less as you are procrastinating to a far lesser degree than if you were not doing time management

Tips to improve time management skills

Remember that time is consumed each day irrespective of whether you use it or not. Time gets spent by thoughts, actions, and conversations. It is important that you are consciously aware of how each of these elements is being used by you and therefore how time is being used. Here are a few techniques to manage time better than you are doing now:

For about a week, carry a notebook along with you wherever you go and record every activity you do and the duration of time the activity took. It may appear tedious initially. But, in a day or two, you will become great at noting down every thought, action, and conversation you had and how much time was used by you during each of these activities.

Once you have this data for about a week, sit down and analyze how much of the time that you spent actually resulted in productive work. You will be amazed at the amount of time that is unwittingly wasted on doing completely unnecessary tasks.

Any activity that is important to you and/or those that give you productive results must be allocated sufficient time during the day. You must create to-do lists that are workable and feasible and not create for the sake of making the list. Create spaces in your appointment for work in the order of priority.

Give a specific time period for each task and be disciplined about completing the task within the given time period. Be realistic about how much time each task will take. Do not underestimate or overestimate the time taken. With practice and experience, you will learn the art of creating great schedules and sticking to them in a disciplined manner.

Ensure that at least half of the time you have allocated for all the tasks is used up for productive purposes depending on your work and personal life.

It is very important that you include sufficient time for breaks and interruptions. It would be foolhardy not to have restorative breaks during the day. You will burn out and nothing will get accomplished. Just remember to keep these breaks realistic.

Make sure you keep about half an hour at the beginning of the day to plan and prioritize your day. Similarly, at the end of the day, ensure you have gone through the schedule you made and tick off things you completely and leave the uncompleted tasks unchecked so that you can include it for the next day.

Do not hesitate to put off all distracting electronic devices such as mobile phones and social media notifications when you are focused on something really important. In fact, I would suggest that you turn them off during critical tasks.

Learn to say no to people or tasks that you simply cannot do. Do not feel guilty or bad for it. If your best friend calls you for a drink and you know you have to start off an important activity in the next five minutes, be upfront with your friend and learn to say no.

Learning to say no doesn't necessarily have to be for drinks. Even if someone asks you for help but you are certain that you cannot provide the help or at least not in the time frame the person wants it in, be honest and learn to say no!

Another aspect of great time management skills is being physically fit. For this, you must ensure that you get a good night's rest and eat nutritious healthy meals. A regular exercise regime will also be very useful as a healthy body houses a healthy mind which, in turn, will help you manage your life better.

The 3...2...1 trick and time management techniques

Creating a schedule is one thing and implementing it is quite another thing. This is where the 3... 2...1 trick will come of use to you. Every task that you have scheduled might not be interesting to you. Yet, you have made that to-do list based on a priority basis. There are bound to be annoying tasks that you do not like on your to-do list.

Now, the time to do that task #4 (which is rather unpleasant for you) has come and you are looking at the list and the following thought is running through your head, "Let me reschedule this and do task # 6 instead." Now, stop this thought right on its track and count 3...2...1. When you reach one, drop the list you are holding and the thought of wanting to restructure and start doing task #4.

You complete task #4 like this and then you realize tasks 5 and 6 are fine. You do them without much ado and then comes task #7, the dreaded one for the day. So, again you look at the list and the restructuring thought enters your head. Immediately you put a stop to that thought and count 3...2...1 and when you reach 1, drop the list and start off doing task #7. And carry on like this until the list is complete.

Sooner than later, you will realize that this 3...2...1 trick is getting deeply imbibed into your system such that it cannot be rooted out at all. It will become a habit that you will learn to love and put into action. In fact, there will come at a time when the 3...2...1 trick will come to you unconsciously every time your mind wants to procrastinate and then you will truly be free from this menace.

CHAPTER 5: GENERAL TIPS TO OVERCOME PROCRASTINATION

By diligently and unfailingly practicing the 3...2...1 trick for about 2 weeks, it will become deeply ingrained in your psyche. Your body and mind will work in sync with each other in such a way that the instant your mind starts counting backward, your body is ready to drop everything at the count of 1 to do what the task at hand.

When this stage is reached, you can start using other useful tips on how to improve your ability to overcome procrastination and achieve more and more success. So, this chapter is dedicated to giving you some great tips that will be easy to follow once you have mastered the 3...2...1 trick.

Avoid blowing the importance of any task out of proportion

Stop treating tasks with more respect than they deserve. For example, you know you need to get a presentation ready by the end of the week. Use the 3...2...1 trick to start off and work on it in a calm and restful manner. Don't treat that presentation as the be-all and end-all of your career. If you do this, you are actually adding unnecessary stress on yourself that will make the task appear even more difficult than it actually is making you want to procrastinate.

Do not be obsessed by perfection

This point has already been discussed as a cause for procrastination. Beware of this attitude and avoid trying to achieve perfection. Remember perfection is highly relative. What I see as perfect need not be seen as perfect by somebody else. Moreover, putting off work for the fear of not achieving perfection is quite naïve because imperfect something is any day better than perfect nothing.

Change your way of thinking – think 'I choose to' instead of 'I have to'

When your spouse to telling you that the lawn needs to be mowed and you tell yourself that 'you have to do it' because your spouse is asking you to do. With this thought, you will find multiple ways to procrastinate including watching TV, playing video games with your children, or taking the dog for a walk. While all these activities could be great for family bonding because you are spending *q*uality time with your children, the mowing of the lawn is important too, isn't it?

So, don't tell yourself 'you have to' to mow the lawn. Tell yourself, "'I choose to' mow the lawn because this is my home and I want it to be beautiful." And then, say 3...2...1

and when you reach 1, take the lawn mower out and get to work.

Reward yourself whenever you finish a task that you would normally procrastinate

Let us take the above example. You chose to mow the lawn and used the 3...2...1 trick and finished it as promised. Now, don't hesitate yourself by playing that favorite video game of yours. Your spouse will not find fault because you have chosen to and finished mowing the lawn and you will find a sense of satisfaction of having earned the reward.

Even before you choose to do a task that you would normally procrastinate, promise yourself a reward that you desire. It could be anything; that delicious brownie in the fridge, that great pair of shoes, time with friends, etc. Just remember to be realistic and ensure that the reward you give yourself is commensurate to the work that you completed.

Do not hesitate to politely get rid of overstaying visitors

If you notice, a large part of your time is taken up by people who cannot complete their own tasks on time. There are many people you will come across who will dilly-dally in a conversation or in a team task to an unrealistic extent. You have to be careful and discern the true procrastinator from one who is, perhaps, slow at conversing.

When you are sure the person belongs to the former category, do the following to ensure your time is not wasted:

Take control of the way the conversation is progressing.

Look at your watch and say that you are already late for an appointment

Politely excuse yourself and walk away from such time-consuming needless conversations

Block off certain hours during the day when you need to work on an important project

There will always be certain projects that each of us are involved in. These highly critical projects keep happening and one follows the other almost seamlessly. You have to allocate certain hours of the day when you block off everything else from your life to work on these critical things. During that time block, don't take appointments, don't go out socializing, don't accept invitations, etc

This important project can be anything. It could be something at office or it could be something at home. When this project comes into your life, set aside blocks of time regularly that will be dedicated to this alone!

Don't wait for the 'right mood'

Waiting for the right frame of mind is a common excuse used by many procrastinators. Be wary of this excuse and when you know that something has to be done, simply count 3...2...1 and drop everything else and do it. The 'right mood' will come sooner than you realize as you involve yourself in the task.

Ask yourself some pertinent questions before you choose to do a task

These pertinent will help you understand if the task that you are planning to take up is really important to be done at the point in time or not. Here are the questions you have to ask yourself:

Are you making the best use of my time by doing this work?

Are you the only person to do this task or can someone else do a better job than me?

Are you using the excuse of doing this task simply to procrastinate a more important but unpleasant job?

Your honest answers to the above questions will easily let you know of your true intentions. These questions will steer you to the right path and ensure that you are doing the right task at the right time.

Be conscious of the schedule you made in the time management chapter

I have told you earlier that creating the schedule is one thing and implementing it is another thing. Be conscious of that schedule and ensure you stick to it as much as possible without deliberately avoiding some jobs in that list that you don't like. If you come across a task you don't like, ask yourself those pertinent questions mentioned in the previous point and when you are certain that you are thinking of procrastinating, stop the thought and count 3... 2...1 and start off your work.

Set a penalty for failures

Just like how you chose to reward yourself for having completed a task without procrastinating, set yourself a penalty if you fail in this aspect. For example, suppose you are a writer and you have chosen to write at least 1000 words a day towards completing your novel. Now, on a particular day, for whatever reason, you do not complete the targeted

1000 words. Put $10 in a box and at the end of the month, donate it to someone or a charity you don't like or don't follow. This will help you stick to your schedule. I would like to point out that being honest with yourself is critical in making these rewards and penalties to work in your favor.

So, every time you feel the resistance of procrastination, use of the above tips and count 3...2...1 and start off.

CHAPTER 6: PROCRASTINATION AND YOU

Procrastination means putting something off until later. It refers to the task that you have to do, or should do, but you do not feel like doing right now. The old joke "Why bother today with what can conveniently be put off until tomorrow" is a fair summary of procrastination. In the world we live in it is common to put things off. None of us enjoys starting to do something we do not like and the mind is really adept at coming up with reasons for not doing something. In many cases it suggests that almost anything else would be a better idea: have a cup of coffee, watch TV, phone a friend, check my email there seems to be a virtually unlimited set of ideas that the mind

can create as a better idea. The darn thing really is lazy; except of course when it comes to inventing reasons for not doing something. In that case it happily works overtime.

It has been suggested that women are more inclined to

procrastinate than men. I do not agree with this: it seems to me that rather than acting at once, many women tend to talk over problems and issues with a close friend, then perhaps go on to discuss them with a small network of people. In so doing they listen to a variety of views before they come to a conclusion on what might be the best course of action. This takes time. Many men on the other hand tend to think about a problem on their own and then reach a decision, without benefit of the views of a support group. In this limited sense of not jumping in feet first it might seem that women "procrastinate" more, but this delay is for the most sensible of reasons. This is really not procrastination but consultation and information gathering, both of which are desirable and positively encouraged in both business and government.

Why start by considering procrastination? It seems sensible to do this before turning to motivation. If you can figure out the reasons why you are putting things off then there is a good chance that you will be able to tackle these reasons and so successfully deal with the problem. Attacking the symptoms rather than the disease may temporarily cover up pain but does not get to the root of the trouble. The things that can work to motivate you best are likely to be those that deal with the reasons for your tendency to procrastinate.

Procrastination is, or can easily become, a habit. If you are a serial procrastinator then it is not just a habit but it is a bad habit. All habits are hard to change - that is why they are called habits. Some habits are good, like cleaning your teeth; others are bad, like picking your nose in public. Habits are just something that we do and we normally do not really think about them, at least until it is too late when regrets might set in. There is not likely to be a simple and instant fix that will suit everybody and instantly cure the habit of procrastination. It is something that will need working at and it might well involve life-style changes, perhaps even major ones. This may seem a daunting prospect but remember: once you have begun to strengthen your motivation then the task of changing yourself becomes easier, certainly easier than it probably now appears.

You might be able to totally stop yourself from being a procrastinator. If you manage it, good! However, it might be that you never absolutely overcome the habit of procrastinating but that does not matter. As long as you do it less often and do it less for the things that are more important to you then this would represent a major improvement on your present situation. You can feel good about this, for you have become a better person.

Why is procrastination bad?

The immediate answer is that jobs do not get done; or they do not get done on time; or they get done on time but they are of lower quality than they might be.

But this is only the beginning for there may be many other bad consequences such as:

- It can make you worry, which increases your level

of stress. This increases the pressure on your health so you might get sick more often. It can even drive you into the deeper and darker realms of depression.

- You might well feel guilty about this habit. You might even feel slightly disgusted with yourself for not doing better or being a better person. Procrastinators often tend to be self-critical.

- If you keep putting things off others will notice and you will get a reputation for being unreliable and untrustworthy.

- Procrastinators might miss out on valuable skill training courses, either because their reputation means they are not selected or, more simply, they fail to apply in time. The result? They are likely to have to put up with a less success in their job and a lower income for life.

- Not attending such courses means that you also lose the chance of meeting people and indulging in networking and this can be an important barrier to your progress.

- You will not receive good evaluations and will lose out on promotions at work.

- You will not get a great recommendation when you leave or apply for a better job elsewhere. In the competitive world we live in, a mediocre reference loses out to a good one.

- Procrastination reinforces itself so putting things off can become a way of life for you.

Why people procrastinate
There are many possible reasons and I can only list a few of them. It is worth reading slowly and thinking about each for a few seconds. Has this one ever applied to you? Does it often apply to you? Considering such matters now can help you later on when you come to do something about your particular problems.

So why might people put things off?

- Maybe innate laziness or a strong preference for avoiding hard work and effort. This does not refer only to physical work, for thinking can be particularly hard and tiring.
- They were not trained as a child to tackle things that they did not really want to do and they have never learned how to do this for themselves.
- They are bad at time management and deciding how long to allocate to a certain task; they might, for example, tend to underestimate the time needed for preparing and writing a good academic paper.
- They do not make a list of what they need to do, either that day, or over the foreseeable future. Note that when completing a task on a list, crossing it off can give a sense of achievement and

self-worth. This can help to improve your motivation.

- They are not good at prioritizing so that even if they make a list they cannot sort out which is urgent and which is important; both of these matter but the things that are urgent should be done first.
- They do not actually read the list or read it often enough; or maybe they fail to stick to it.
- They are rebellious, hate being told what to do and dislike scheduling, even by themselves.
- They are trying to punish someone; they do not start something they should do because they feel "that will teach them".
- They are stressed out and lack the energy to tackle anything much.
- They feel overwhelmed by the magnitude of what faces them and do not know where to begin.
- They sit and worry rather than starting; time spent worrying is not time spent either thinking or doing.
- They know little or nothing about the task facing them and feel incapable of making a start.
- They feel that the topic or job is boring and it is simply not for them.
- They have a dream but they feel that they do not really deserve it. Or it remains in the land of day dreams.

- Some people fear success and what problems it might entail for them in the future; deep down they are perhaps satisfied with what they have.
- A few may seek perfectionism and as they feel that they cannot achieve their impossibly high standards they feel incapable of beginning.
- Some hate reading their own work and editing it for improvement.
- For many people their mind tends to wander and consider almost anything but the task facing them so a start is not made. It is easy to be distracted from the task in hand or not even in hand yet.
- Their intentions are not strongly based and they have a weak feeling that they should do more but that is all.
- "I'm not in the mood". Some persuade themselves that they have to be in the right mood to do something; this always tends to be sometime in the future rather than now.
- Excuses become the norm. When one has developed the habit of making excuses one tends to believe them; and a good excuse for putting something off can always be invented.
- An interesting theoretical explanation is "slow thinking" versus "fast thinking". Slow thinking refers to a deliberate consideration of things that would be good for us, such as going to the gym for exercise or eating less if we are overweight. The

process requires effort , self-discipline and can be tiring. Fast thinking on the other hand is making a quick decision to do something enjoyable, like buying something on impulse at a supermarket checkout. We sign up for gym membership as a result of slow thinking; after having done so we then rarely go and instead choose to watch TV, play computer games, or whatever, as fast thinking wins out. Human beings exhibit both modes of thinking.

And so the list goes on. The reason for presenting you with such a long list is that if you are to overcome your problem of procrastination it is essential that you begin to understand why you might tend to put things off. Only when you begin to see at least some of the reasons that you do this can you tackle your own individual problem in an effective manner. It is far more sensible to fix the reason for your problem than to try to apply a solution that would actually fit a different reason.

Are you a procrastinator?

Some who are might well deny it, partly because they are not much given to self analysis and have not thought about it; and partly because having considered it they fail to recognize it in themselves. Perhaps it interferes with the self image they hold.

Some people seem to be unwilling to admit that they have a problem or are less than perfect. I have heard people say that they prefer to put things off until the last minute because they work better under pressure but in many cases I feel that this is self delusion.

If you can answer yes to a few of the following **q**uestions you probably procrastinate.

- I read my emails but do not answer them, or file them away, or delete them. I let them clutter up my inbox until time renders a lot of them out of date.
- When I am working on something I stop to check for emails every few minutes.
- I do not buy Christmas or birthday presents until the last minute then have to race around the stores looking at empty shelves or racks of rejects.
- I do not pay bills on time even when I have the money.
- I am sometimes late with an income tax return.
- I have not always cashed gift certificates or book tokens that have a cut-off date and so lost them.

The best way, indeed the only way, to tackle the problem of procrastination is to increase your desire to get on with things, to make a start and enjoy it. You have to change your patterns of behaviour and this means strengthening your motivation and self-motivation. So let's turn to that now.

CHAPTER 7: 39 ACTIONABLE TIPS TO INCREASE PRODUCTIVITY INSTANTLY AND STOP PROCRASTINATION!

1. Wake up earlier

There seems to be a universal perspective that there is not enough time in a day. We hear it over and over again. Nowadays, we are busier than ever, whether you're a parent with a full- time job and driving your kids to soccer games, a millennial attending university while balancing extracurricular activities, someone looking for more work-life balance, or everyone else in between.

Whether you wake up an hour earlier or even more, starting off your day by working on something for YOURSELF feels very empowering because when we do that, we are waking up for ourselves, not for anybody else.

Use this time to work on whatever task or goal you are looking to accomplish. It could be a personal project, a work-related task, or working on losing those ten pounds that you said you would lose six months ago.

Studies have shown that our willpower is like a battery. It's 100 percent full in the morning, but it drains slowly throughout the day with each individual task or interaction we have. By waking up earlier, you ensure that you devote that chunk of time and energy to something that is just for you, not anybody else. This is HUGE.

Start implementing this strategy in your life and it will do wonders. Trust me.

2. Create a morning ritual (You've woken up early. Great. Now what?)

If your schedule is packed, create a morning ritual to boost your daily productivity. Plan your ritual so that you will conquer every day. You can do this the night before so that you're not wasting any time in the morning.

For example, here is my morning ritual:

1. Wake up—don't hit the snooze button. We'll talk about that later.
2. Brush my teeth
3. Exercise
4. Shower
5. Meditate/be thankful for all the people and things in my life
6. Get dressed

7. Eat breakfast
8. Read
9. Work on projects

Everyone's ritual will be individualized and personal, but you get what I mean. Creating a set schedule takes out any guesswork and lets you focus on what is most important.

3. Avoid any "screen time"

You will notice that I didn't include "check my phone" or "check email" on my morning ritual items. There's a reason for that.

On the days that I didn't hit the snooze button, picking up my phone used to be the first thing I would do in the morning. I would check work emails, personal emails, stock-market news, Facebook feeds, Instagram posts, and before you knew it, an hour had passed by before I even brushed my teeth.

That did not leave any time to work on anything for my own personal development or my personal goals. Instead of following this bad example, create and follow your ritual plan (like mine under #2 above). Your productivity will skyrocket and provide you a great sense of accomplishment.

4. Exercise

If you're thinking, "I'm already waking up early … now you're telling me to exercise on top of that?!", it's a fair *q*uestion. I used to be a night owl and was allergic to mornings, but now that we have two children, I'm the opposite. If you go to the gym after work or do a run during your lunchtime, that's great! All I'm saying is that studies have shown that exercise has a ton of benefits to your productivity (info gathered at www.lifehack.org).

- You will have more energy.

By exercising in the morning, you will have more energy throughout your day. It will release endorphins to make you feel good, reduce stress, and clear your mind, and it gives you a great sense of accomplishment to begin your day. I would say it's equally beneficial to your physical health as your mental health.

- You will feel empowered.

Like I said, beginning your day feeling a great sense of accomplishment is priceless. It makes you feel and BELIEVE that you are in control of your life, and it positively affects your attitude and decisions for the rest of the day.

- You will be more productive.

By having a clear mind and being in the right mindset, your stress levels will be lower, and you will have fewer distractions, which will provide you a clear path to productivity.

Now, I know that telling yourself to exercise is easy, but the act of doing it is not. If it was easy, everybody would be running around with bodies like Zac Efron and Jessica Alba, but unfortunately that's not the case.

Here are some tips to con**q**uer the two hardest parts of exercising in the morning: waking up and getting yourself to the gym.

Waking up

As I mentioned in the earlier, I was a notorious snooze-button hitter. I hit that button more times than a contestant on Family Feud. So what did I do to change this? Here are a few options you can try:

- Set the alarm for the time you want to get up—and I'm talking about the EXACT time, not ten or twenty minutes earlier, but the EXACT time. Then place the alarm, or your phone, on the opposite side of your room.
- Once you're up and zombie walk to your alarm, you'll increase the chances tenfold of starting your day instead of going back to sleep.
- Use an alarm app. There are some good alarm apps out there to help you wake up in the morning, but a great one is "The Rock Clock" (which is free for Apple and Android devices) developed by movie star Dwayne "The Rock" Johnson's company 7 Bucks Productions. Along with setting an alarm, this motivational app allows you to enter a personal goal that displays each morning when the alarm sounds on your phone and includes motivational messages to

inspire you. Oh ... and one more thing—there is no snooze button!

Any one of these will do. Just choose the one that works best for you that makes you get up each morning excited to conquer the day!

Getting yourself to the gym

- Lay out your gym clothes and pack your gym bag the night before and leave it right by your bed along with your car keys. You'll wake up, pick up the bag, and go.
- If you don't have a gym membership, you can do a home workout instead. I choose my workout the night before and write it down so that I'm not wasting time in the morning, trying to decide what workout to do while I'm half-asleep. Again, lay out your workout clothes the night before so that you can help your morning self-succeed.
- Note that it doesn't have to be a long workout either. My home workouts take anywhere from fifteen to thirty minutes each day, and they help me clear my mind and reduce stress.

If you're looking for some home workout recommendations, there are a ton of great ones on Youtube. Just search for "home workout without equipment" or better yet, just click here.

You'll notice a theme here: the path of least resistance. The goal is to eliminate the majority of (or all) the obstacles in the way (that you control) of achieving your end goal, which leads to more productivity in less time. Who doesn't want that?

5. Eat breakfast

Breakfast is truly the most important meal of the day. After fasting for the past eight hours (or however long you slept), your body is craving to be fed.

Decide what you're going to eat for breakfast the night before (or meal prep on Sunday for the week) so that you're not wasting any time deciding "Should I have eggs this morning? Or cereal?"

It's the path of least resistance, folks!

6. Meditation

You can meditate anytime of the day, but I include it in my morning ritual and occasionally at night just before bedtime. This is very important in my opinion, and it may come easier to some than others.

Honestly, I am not a spiritual person, so initially the thought of meditation was a little uncomfortable for me until I realized that it didn't have to be overwhelming. Meditating doesn't mean you have to be "one with the universe" or sit cross-legged on a pillow. It's definitely much more than that.

If you're not sure where to get started, I recommend an app called HeadSpace. It walks you through clearing your mind with a calm, soothing voice guiding you, and it's simple to use. This was the tool I first used when I began meditating during a stressful part of my life, and it definitely helped.

Meditation clears your mind, slows down your heartbeat, and provides a ton of benefits for your mental and physical well-being.

According to theartofliving.org, here are a list of its benefits:

On a physical level, meditation:

- Lowers high blood pressure
- Lowers the levels of blood lactate, reducing anxiety attacks
- Decreases any tension-related pain, such as tension headaches, ulcers, insomnia, muscle and joint problems
- Increases serotonin production that improves mood and behavior
- Improves the immune system
- Increases the energy level, as you gain an inner source of energy

Meditation also lets you rejuvenate and allows you to focus and make decisions with a clear mind. With regular practice of meditation:

- Anxiety decreases
- Emotional stability improves
- Creativity increases
- Happiness increases
- Intuition develops
- Gain clarity and peace of mind
- Problems become smaller
- Meditation sharpens the mind by gaining focus and expands through relaxation
- A sharp mind without expansion causes tension, anger, and frustration
- An expanded consciousness without sharpness can lead to lack of action/progress
- The balance of a sharp mind and an expanded consciousness brings perfection

Meditation doesn't have to be time-consuming. We are all very busy people, but making the investment to heal your mind will pay dividends throughout the day and exponentially throughout your life.

For me, meditation is taking five to ten minutes every morning to clear my mind and then thinking of at least one thing in my life that I'm thankful for. It really puts me in a peaceful state, and expressing gratitude for the people or things in my life that I love puts me in a happy and appreciative mindset. It reduces stress and helps me focus on the important things I want to accomplish in the day and in my life.

7. Express gratitude

As I just mentioned, self-improvement gurus like Lewis Howes talk about expressing gratitude all the time. It allows you to reflect on what you've accomplished and what you want to accomplish and puts your mind in the right state. It also allows you to take a step back and get perspective on your life.

For the person with a tight deadline at the end of the week, expressing gratitude for their health, their loved ones, and anything else they cherish will take the stress off and allow them to complete their work in the right frame of mind.

This is a great practice for not allowing you to take things for granted. I watched a YouTube video from Fight-Mediocrity which helped me begin this practice.

In one of his videos, the narrator states that we should all realize that we've won the lottery already. Anyone with a clean bill of health should consider themselves the luckiest person in the world. Imagine how much someone with a critical illness would give to be in your shoes. Or if you have your full eyesight, how much would a blind person be willing to spend to see what you see? It would be priceless. Be thankful for what you already have instead of focusing on the things that you don't.

Instead of waking up, rushing to work, and living every day like we're a program from the Matrix, think about what you want to accomplish during the day and what will fulfill you. "Stop acting like you live twice" is an anonymous *q*uote that really stuck with me.

Rather than just checking emails and going to meetings, this action will put you in the right mindset to help you accomplish what's most important to you throughout the day.

8. Make your bed

It sounds like a strange tip, right? That's what I thought too until I started implementing this in my everyday life. Charles Duhigg, the author of The Power of Habit, says that the quick, simple task of making your bed can help increase productivity for the rest of the day.

Think it sounds like a bunch of mumbo jumbo? Well let's think about it. Completing a task, no matter how miniscule we think it may be, provides us a sense of accomplishment. It gives us a good feeling, and we're more likely to keep that momentum going throughout the day to prolong that feeling.

So instead of thinking of it as "just making your bed", think of it as beginning a snowball effect that will gain more and more momentum throughout the day.

Duhigg puts it more elo*q*uently: "A keystone habit can spark chain reactions that help other good habits take hold".

Preach, brother!

9. If you're thinking about it, DO IT!

I truly think if you follow this rule, you'll never be lazy again in your life. How many times have you thought "I'll do those dishes later" or "I'll take out the trash later" and so on, and so on, and so on? I used to be that guy! And trust me, my girlfriend at the time did not appreciate it.

For you readers that are "that guy" or "that gal", do yourself and the people around you a favor, and like Nike's slogan says, "Just Do It!" And if it's a bigger task or a project, then "Just Start it!" It sounds like common sense, but common sense isn't always common practice. This is the simplest advice that we already know, yet the majority of us don't implement it.

Nobody has achieved success by sitting back, overanalyzing, or waiting for the perfect time. Successful, productive individuals will always tell you that it all starts with taking action. It's like going to the gym. The toughest part is getting there, and you'll thank yourself when you do.

By the way, I implemented this tip into my life and that girlfriend I mentioned above is now my wife. Coincidence? I think not.

10. What would make today great?

Another tip that you can implement right away is to put some thought into what would make your day great. What are the things that need to be done throughout the day that will make it have meaning and provide you a sense of accomplishment?

It can be anything from taking the stairs instead of the elevator to writing 2,000 words in your blog post. No matter what it is, make it attainable and realistic. Going to the gym and working on cardio is realistic. Losing five pounds in a day is not.

You can write it down or have it at the back of your mind throughout the day. Doing this will make you more likely to focus on these goals than if you hadn't practiced this.

How many times have your days been consumed by meetings and responding to emails? Before you know it, the day is done and you haven't accomplished what you wanted? More than likely, you did not put enough thought into what your key goals were for the day.

I was guilty of this for years at my corporate position. Once I made the mindset switch, I was more productive than ever.

11. Monitor your current time use baseline

If you don't feel like you're as productive as you want to be, or if you feel like there's not enough time in the day, try noting down all your daily actions in detail. This will show you which activities were productive and which weren't. It will also give you a bird's-eye view of your day, which is a perspective we rarely see for ourselves.

This activity gives us the data that will allow us to eliminate our nonproductive behavior while allowing us to add to our productiveness and our most productive times. For example, when I initially practiced this exercise, I noticed that my most productive hours were from 9:00 to 11:00 a.m. (before I started thinking about lunch) and from 3:00 to 5:00 p.m. I would schedule in my most demanding tasks during these times because I knew I would get more done during my "peak" productivity hours.

Everybody is different, so give this a try to see which hours are the most effective for you.

12. Eliminate (not avoid) distractions

Our world is full of distractions. Technology has provided us all the tools we need to communicate and keep in touch with each other, which is fantastic ... but not all the time.

How many times have you seen a notification on your phone while you were working? You pick up your phone, check your notification, check your email, check the photo your friends tagged you on Instagram, and so on, and so on, and so on. There goes thirty minutes or more that you could have used to put towards your important work.

The next time you're focused on a task, try shutting down your phone completely. I know some of your hearts just skipped a beat at the mere thought of that, but seriously try it. After the initial shock, you will be surprised how much you get done. Putting your phone in airplane mode will also work if you can't lay your phone to rest for an hour or so.

Now I understand if you have kids or a spouse and you

would like to keep your phone on for family emergency calls, so there are some other recommendations you can use to eliminate these distractions:

1. Place it outside the room where you are working (if possible) or in your bag or purse. Out of sight, out of mind.
2. Turn off your app notifications. We easily get distracted by that flashing light on our phone or the little orange icon on your apps showing you how many notifications you have on social media. Turn off the notifications to eliminate this.

Computer tips

If you're working on your PC or Mac and don't want to be distracted, close down all the applications other than the one you're working in. We are all guilty of interrupting our work to check emails just because we see a pop-up notification. Or we're reading an article that leads to clicking on another, and before we know it, we have fifty tabs open in our Internet browser. Closing all other applications will eliminate these distractions.

If you feel like you need help with this like many do, there is an application called Freedom that blocks apps, websites, or the entire Internet on iPhones, iPads, Windows, and Mac computers, which allows you to be more productive. You can program which websites you want to block out and for how long, and the only way to access it before the set time limit is to restart your PC or phone. It's a very useful tool for the noisy world we live in.

13. Learn to say NO

Distractions don't always come in the form of technology. They can also come in the form of requests from others, whether it be a meeting or something that someone needs assistance with. In my personal opinion, "people" distractions are harder to deal with than technological distractions.

With technology, you can just shut it down or completely ignore it, and you won't hurt its feelings. People, on the other hand, are more sensitive and trickier to deal with.

Think of it like you have a fixed quota for the number of times you can say YES each day. Each time you say "yes" to someone else, you're going to have to say NO to a commitment you've made to yourself. It's very important that you get good at this skill in order to accomplish the tasks and goals on your checklist instead of ticking them off someone else's.

Also when you do say "no," make it firm so that it doesn't leave the door open for a "maybe" or "next week". If you don't make it firm, you will have to go through the process all over again.

Before I adopted this mindset, I used to feel guilty or unhelpful, but there are positive ways to say "no".

When I used to work in the corporate world, one of my colleagues asked me to complete a task for them that I had the knowledge and experience to do. I had a lot on my plate and deadlines to meet, so I told them that I wasn't able to assist them due to my schedule; however, I sent them a document I had previously created that provided a step-by-step process on how to resolve their request.

In this example, even though I said no, I made it a positive by providing another helpful resource to assist them.

14. Delegate

One of my friends received a parking ticket for $90 that he thought he didn't deserve. He spent all day in court to wait for his hearing and fought the ticket. In the end he had the fee reduced by half, but he missed out on a full day of work. His hourly rate was $50, so in actuality, instead of making $45 by spending all day in court, he lost $400 by not going to work. To my math, that's a $355 loss for the day.

That's an extreme example, but the point is, time is literally money.

If you're working on a personal project, you can hire a virtual assistant. There are a bunch of websites out there such as Fiverr, where you can find someone who can complete a simple, time-consuming task for you while you focus on the important things in your life.

Oftentimes when people are just starting out, people make the mistake of saying, "I don't delegate because it takes just as long to explain it than to do it myself".

Yes, that may be true, but you won't be delegating just

this one time. The old adage "Give a man a fish, he eats for a day; teach a man to fish, and he eats for a lifetime" has never been truer.

If you're going to be productive, you have to be good at delegation. I'm a big believer of your time is money, and you can't do everything on your own. Sometimes it makes more financial sense to hire someone to complete a task rather than to complete it yourself.

15. Make a to-do list

But not just any to-do list. Include items or tasks that you've been avoiding, not just the ones that you know you will complete. After you've written them down, set deadlines for them so that you have some urgency to complete them.

A great tool I use is an app called Todoist. It allows you to write out your daily tasks, as well as your long-term tasks, and it makes you set a deadline for each one. You also receive daily reminders for your upcoming tasks to keep you in check.

You can also create separate projects with to-do lists within each category. For example, if you have a vehicle category, you can set items such as wash car, get an oil change, renew registration, etc.

It's a very simple yet very powerful tool that has definitely increased my productivity.

16. Reward yourself!

This one's my favorite for obvious reasons. Of course, we all need to work hard and work smart to be productive, but you can't go 100 miles an hour all the time. That's just not realistic —you'll get burnt out.

Taking a break or rewarding yourself will also rejuvenate you and give you the push you need to strive on.

Even movie star Dwayne "The Rock" Johnson has cheat days after spending countless hours at the gym each week.

The reward will also motivate you when you're in the thick of it to complete the task or reach the goal.

17. Focus on the end goal

This is another tip you can use the next time you're struggling to complete your task or reach your goal. Sometimes we get lost in the grind and forget the very reason we're working on a certain task. Your perspective isn't clear when you're in this mindset. Instead, focus on the end goal and the reason you're doing what you're doing.

For instance, when you're at the gym doing 100 sit-ups, it's not going to be fun and you may want to quit. If you think only about the present task, you likely won't be motivated to follow through. However, if you think about the future end goals (for example, looking good and feeling confident for your upcoming beach vacation), you will become more motivated and more likely to complete the short-term task.

Big or long-term projects may feel like a grind at times. This may cause you to stray from doing the work you're supposed to do and to get sidetracked. Focus on the end goal, especially on those tough days, because it will recharge you to go forward.

18. Be accountable

So you've added an item to your to-do list. Check! You've added a deadline to your item. Check!

Next step is to complete the item. Check?

Listen, we're all human, and just because we write something down doesn't mean we're going to do it. I know firsthand as a former notorious procrastinator that your brain will tell you, "It's okay. I'll do it tomorrow" or "It wasn't that important anyways".

If you're the only one aware that it's on your to-do list, disappointing yourself may not seem so bad in the short term since you'd rather watch Game of Thrones at the time. We often choose instant gratification over long-term term success because ... well ... let's face it, it's just easier.

My recommendation for this would be to get an accountability partner, someone who will help keep you honest for your must-do commitments. They will provide you encouragement when you need it and that extra push to help you keep moving forward.

Tell your partner, friend, or family member about a goal you're setting out to do. Psychologists have found that saying something out loud makes it more real and we're more likely to follow through with it, especially if we've said it to someone who will ask about it down the road.

Running partners often do this to make sure they wake up and complete their run. It could be as little as someone sending you a text to ask how your project is going or if you exercised yet today. Nobody wants to disappoint someone they care about.

19. The 2-minute rule

This is another piece of advice I wish I had followed earlier than I did. If it takes less than two minutes, then just do it!

David Allen, the author of Getting Things Done, provides an example of this when he talks about his email management. When a message arrives in David's mailbox, he decides if he can deal with it in two minutes or less by responding or deleting the message. This will definitely help you "Inbox Zero" enthusiasts and those of you who have a tough time managing email.

Of course, this can obviously be applied to everyday life with housework or anything that you feel would fit this mold.

20. Don't be a perfectionist

One of my favorite quotes is "Progress beats perfection every time". That couldn't be more true.

The perfect idea, perfect situation, or perfect time will likely never come. There will always be another commitment or another event in your life that will deter you from achieving your goal. Life is messy. Life is busy. Deal with it.

If you're waiting for the perfect moment or not completing something because it's not perfect, you will definitely fall behind the pack. You just need to complete it and move on to the next task.

21. Take it one task at a time

With so much to do in our busy lives, we constantly multitask and think we're being more productive, but in actuality our work may suffer from that.

When I started writing, I would start with an idea and write down a few hundred words. Then I would think of another topic that I thought would also be interesting to write about, so I would start a draft on that topic as well. And then another idea would pop into my head, and so on. I would go back and forth, thinking that I could accomplish more since I was working on three articles at once, but in actuality, my work suffered due to this.

I noticed when I sat down and focused on one article at a time that not only was I more efficient, but the quality of my work doubled.

Don't get me wrong—multitasking is much needed for smaller tasks, but if you're working on a large project or goal, your full, undivided attention will get you to the finish line faster and with better results.

22. Change your environment

Is your work environment optimized for productivity? Does it encourage you to get things done, or are there distractions that can deter you from your work?

During my first year of university, I would do my homework and study in my room. You know what else was in my room? A computer that I used to browse the web and to chat with my friends on MSN Messenger (yes, I'm dating myself here). And you guessed it ... I had a terrible GPA that year.

I knew I had to make a change if I wanted to improve my grades and graduate. When my final grades came in at the end of the semester, it took that rude awakening to show me that my current studying environment was not working.

The next semester I started driving myself to the university library to study. No laptop, no friends, and no distractions. I was able to raise my GPA by two grade levels by the end of the year.

Environment preference varies for everyone. Some prefer a *q*uiet place in their home while others work best sitting at a local coffee shop. Whatever the case, make sure you are comfortable with your surroundings and that you have everything you need within arm's reach. Environment is an important, if not the most important, key to productivity.

23. Hang out with people that motivate you and make you grow

One of the best ways to stop procrastination and improve productivity is interacting with the right people. We all know people that are pessimists that settle in their life and bring down others that have big goals. These could be relatives, friends, or colleagues, but you know who I'm talking about. If possible, you need to cut these people out of your life, and if not, then don't listen to them.

By interacting with others with like-minded goals and thoughts, you gain support, confidence, motivation, and knowledge. Communicating with others to share your experiences adds to your growth as an individual. I am a big believer in self-improvement and that everyone needs it in their life. If you're not growing, you're not moving forward.

If you don't have any of these influences in your life, there are a ton of inspiring people in the world that you can follow off-line through books or online through audiobooks, podcasts, blogs, YouTube, or even Instagram.

An individual that really motivates me is YouTube Vlogger Casey Neistat. He is a filmmaker and software application founder that loves his work and shares it with the world. His motto is "DO MORE," which is tattooed on his arm, and he always spreads the most contagious attitude to his viewers: positivity.

Surround yourself with positivity and you will see positive results. Positivity breeds success; negativity breeds failure.

24. Look for someone who has achieved what you want to achieve.

Sometimes a goal is just a dream we don't act on because we don't feel like it can be accomplished by "someone like me". If you are one of those individuals with this mindset, you are not alone.

Instead of not beginning to work on your goal, search for people that have done what you're setting out to do. You will realize that these individuals were just like you—someone with a goal that ACTED on it.

"Success is steady progress of one's personal goals." - Jim Rohn

Once you start, you will already be ahead of 99 percent of everybody else that doesn't.

25. Pomodoro technique

This is a time-management method that was developed by Francesco Cirillo in the 1980s. Don't let the fancy name intimidate you. ("Pomodoro" means "tomato" for those of you who don't speak Italian.) Cirillo had a kitchen timer in the shape of a tomato in his university days, which is where the name originated from. Now that you've had your history lesson for the day, what is this technique, and how do you implement it?

At the core of this method is the idea of taking frequent breaks to improve mental agility and endurance. Working three hours straight may be efficient for a select few, but most would burn out, and their work would suffer as a result. Instead, try this.

The next time you're ready to take on a task, work for twenty-five minutes, break for five minutes, then repeat. The idea is that you are most efficient in these twenty-five-minute "bursts" when you can speed through and get things done. It makes you focus on your one task because you have only a limited time to work on it, so your brain pushes you to get it done.

Again, everybody is different, so if you prefer working for longer periods with longer breaks, feel free to do so. The same principle applies.

There are a ton of free Pomodoro apps out there, so you don't need to go through the hassle of setting it up on your smartphone. A couple popular ones are Pomodoro Time (iOS) and Productivity Challenge Timer (Android), which have a large number of positive reviews.

As another suggestion, if you're not sure what to do during those five-minute breaks and are feeling antsy, here are a few suggestions:

- Stand up and stretch; it will reset both your mind and body to loosen you up.
- Walk to the kitchen and grab some water.
- Complete a small, mindless task that takes you only a couple minutes or less, whether it be shredding some papers or washing the dishes if you work from home.

Then get right back into it!

26. Pause and think

We do a lot of the little things every day out of habit, things that may not even be that beneficial to us. We do it because we've always done it. The total of all of these actions throughout the days and weeks may cost you a lot of time that could have been focused in another useful area in your life.

So before you start a task, pause and ask yourself, is this something that really matters? You'll be surprised how many times you'll answer "No" and move on to the next task that actually matters.

I find this really useful in helping me stay focused on my "must-dos" throughout the day so that I can accomplish the most important tasks first and put the "nice to haves" in the backseat.

27. Drink more water

Make a conscious effort to drink enough water throughout the day. Not only does staying well hydrated benefit your health, but it can also provide a number of benefits towards your daily productivity.

Scientific research has shown that drinking water will increase our energy, which we all could use more of when powering through tasks, and it also improves our mood. Even mild dehydration has been shown to have a negative impact on mood.

We've all heard of hunger causing someone to become "hangry"; well, thirst can cause that as well, to a lesser extent. I guess that would be called "thangry"? Drink your water to avoid it.

28. Avoid the sweatpants

This mostly applies to anyone that works remotely or solo-preneurs that don't have to physically interact with anyone else during the day. Dressing up changes your mindset and mood. If you dress differently, then you will act differently.

It will also increase your self-confidence, which is great for any aspect of your life. Think about how you feel when you look at yourself in the morning wearing your baggy T-shirt and sweatpants as opposed to when you're all showered and looking professional. I'm not saying wear a tuxedo or anything, but wear something comfortable that you feel confident in.

29. Group similar tasks together

Before I organized my days and weeks into sections or compartments, my days often felt hectic, and I didn't have any structure, which often led to me feeling like I didn't accomplish enough or what I wanted to by the end of the day.

To combat this, every Sunday I lay out my calendar and create my "perfect week". Meaning, in an ideal world, what would I like to accomplish each day for the entire week, and how would I break it down?

For example, I would break each day of the week into four sections:

1. Morning - Wake up time to the time I start work
2. AM - Work starting time to lunchtime
3. PM - After lunch to the time I leave work
4. Evening - After dinner to bedtime

The morning block would include all the things in my morning ritual that I spoke about earlier in the book, e.g., shower, brush teeth, exercise, meditate, eat breakfast, etc.

For the AM block, I write down the must dos of the day and what I really want to accomplish. I complete these in the morning because I am most productive in the morning, and my focus is at its sharpest.

For example, I typically write in the mornings and schedule time for intellectual growth because those require the most thought from me. Make sure that you eliminate ALL potential distractions and interruptions during this time. Put your phone on silent, place yourself in a great work environment, and just do work.

As stated earlier, think of your willpower as a battery. It's fully charged at 100 percent when you wake up and slowly depletes throughout the day. Working on your most important tasks in the morning guarantees that you will do the things that are most needed and provides you a higher sense of accomplishment by the end of the day.

For the PM block, I typically schedule in meetings and check email. These activities are less demanding on my mind but are still required to be productive.

Lastly, if you choose to include the evening block, you can schedule things like exercise (if you don't have it included in the morning block), reading, or anything you like that helps you unwind for the day. My evening block typically consists of family time, reading, and planning out the next day.

Before I implemented this system into my daily life, I found that I had too much back and forth going on and was not as efficient as I wanted to be. Grouping similar tasks together allows you to get into a rhythm and become more productive and efficient.

You can also group all your "interruptions" together, such as booking off an afternoon for phone calls, external meetings, or answering questions. This will definitely save you time and mental energy.

Hopefully that gives you a better idea of how to compartmentalize your days. This is a very powerful strategy that I found almost doubled my productivity once I started using it.

30. Use your commute time

Whether you walk, bike, use public transportation, or drive your car to work, plenty of things can be done during this precious time. While many complain about the amount of time it takes them to travel to and from work, I actually enjoy this time because I make it productive. If you use public transportation, you can read and answer emails on your smartphone or even work on projects if you bring a laptop.

All commuters could use this time for intellectual growth. Instead of staring out the window and daydreaming, listen to a podcast or audiobook. I've digested an enormous amount of information by listening to dozens of audiobooks just by doing this, which has increased my intellectual growth exponentially.

31. Create a "do not do" list

We've all heard of a to-do list, but few of us have heard of a "do not do" list. On a do-not-do list, write down all the potential things that could come up in your day that could potentially be distractions and deter you away from your must-dos.

It could be anything from not attending any meetings for the entire day, not answering the phone during the morning, not checking Instagram, etc. By implementing this strategy, you gain time simply by not wasting time.

32. Do things right the first time around

There's a saying, "If you're not going to do things right the first time, when are you going to have time to?" Although it may take a little longer to complete a task thoroughly the first time around, chances are it will save you more exponential amounts of time down the road.

Take the example of writing documentation for a process at work that others require. If you're thorough the first time around, you can then pass on that document to others so that they can follow the steps and complete it on their own.

If not done correctly, your colleague(s) will likely come back to ask you questions, and you may have to rewrite the document, which will eat into your scarce commodity, time. However, if it's done correctly the first time around, it will free up much more time down the road.

33. Go against the grain

This is a personal life hack that I've found to be extremely beneficial. Whether it's the grocery store, the gym, or any other location that can get busy, I recommend going during the less busy times and avoiding peak times.

For example, when my wife and I grocery shop on a weekday night, we're in and out in less than thirty minutes. In the past when we went on the weekends, by the time the grocery bags reached our car, we had spent an hour to an hour and a half.

Your time is valuable, especially your personal time. Instead of spending an unnecessary hour in crowded parking lots, aisles, and waiting in line, you could be spending that hour on more productive things and enjoying that time with family.

34. Clear your workspace

Make your workspace tidy. Before you begin your work, take a minute and clear any unnecessary papers or random material off your desk. A messy desk can add anxiety or stress, especially if you're on a tight deadline.

Clean your virtual desktop as well. We're all guilty of saving files to our desktop, never to look at them again, or we have files on there that shouldn't be. Delete what you don't need and move your important files to the correct location. Clearing these documents will help you avoid distractions.

Also, if you have a ton of windows open like I do sometimes, close down what you're not working on to declutter your screen.

A clean workspace allows you to focus on what you want to accomplish without distractions.

35. Play music or background sound

Each person is obviously different, but if you find the sound of silence deafening, any little sound may distract you from your work. Playing soft music will cure this and may get you in the flow of work. If you're like myself and find lyrics to be distracting (yes, sometimes I end up singing along), then find instrumental versions of some of your favorite albums.

If that doesn't work for you, there are plenty of background-sound apps out there that you can download and play while you work. I currently use Relax Melodies to play white noise for my newborn, but working adults can use it too, so don't feel ashamed.

36. Do the hardest or most unappealing task first

Sometimes we push what we need to do the most to the background, typically because it's the most difficult or the most unappealing task. This happens to be one of the main reasons people procrastinate.

So instead of leaving it for the end of the day, or telling yourself that you'll "do it later", do it first thing in the morning. As I mentioned earlier in this book, our willpower is the strongest in the morning, so prioritizing the difficult/unappealing task first will allow you to finally complete it.

Not only do you get the benefit of completing it, it will start a productivity snowball effect for the rest of the day. Most people who use this strategy feel like they can complete any other tasks throughout the day without a problem since they completed the hardest one first.

You'll also feel a sense of accomplishment, which will motivate you to keep pushing forward.

37. Write it down (capture every idea)

It's happened to all of us. We're sitting at our desk working on a task when something triggers our brain with an idea or thought that leads us to open up another application or web browser to work on that idea instead. Thirty minutes go by, and you realize that you haven't been working on your task at hand.

There are applications out there, such as Freedom.to as I mentioned earlier in this book, to stop you from opening up other applications, but if you don't want to lose your thought, just write it down on a text document or with a pen and paper and come back to it after you've completed your task.

This will reduce the distraction of your own thoughts, and you won't be thinking, "What was that idea I had again? Darn … I should've written it down".

38. Write a done list

So we have the to-do list, the do-not-do list, and now we have the "done list".

At the end of each day, write down all the things you accomplished. Humans are instinctively visual learners, and looking at your list of accomplishments for the day can be very powerful. It gives you a sense of pride and motivation for the next day.

Some to-do list apps, such as Todoist, show a "Completed Tasks" section as well.

39. Get inspired

Sometimes we lose motivation, or we don't feel inspired to complete that task or goal we've been working on or haven't even started.

Reading inspirational quotes can give you the kick you need to get off the couch and be productive. I honestly used to think they were corny, but I tracked down some inspirational social media accounts on Instagram that I thought were really motivating when I needed an extra boost. A couple Instagram accounts I follow are @GaryVee (Founder of VaynerMedia), @AgentSteven (no, this is not me), and @before5am. These accounts provide practical motivation that I have found to be thought-provoking and inspiring.

CHAPTER 8: MOTIVATION AND YOU

Almost all babies and toddlers are fired with the urge to learn and explore their immediate surroundings while their brains soak up information like a sponge. It has been claimed that from when someone is born to reaching their second birthday the rate of learning progress is the same as from being two years' old to getting a Ph.D. It may be true and it certainly is a darned impressive claim. Admittedly, as we grow older our rate of learning does slow down. This seems to be an inevitable product of ageing although scientists are reportedly working on a pill for adults which could lead them to replicate the learning ability of a child. If it works we might all become super- people but on the other hand there could be a danger of brain overload and breakdowns. Our brains may not be sufficiently hardwired to take in all this extra information at warp speed. In any case, the ability to learn new things does not slow down all that dramatically as one grows older and it only gets a little harder, at least until old age sets in.

Many adult human beings, but certainly not all, seem to be essentially lazy; but coupled with this they may, somewhat paradoxically, have a desire to perform and do better. It might be they want a good job, wealth (including the ability to buy fashionable clothes, the latest gadgets, foreign holidays etc.), power, to attract sexual partners, or to impress others including their own family and friends.

Something must be driving them or they simply would not bother to strive to do better. Once one has a roof over one's head, clothing to wear, and food on the table one can survive. But most people want more than that so they do try. To dream is one thing but to live the dream requires more than luck. It is more likely to happen if you possess some innate inability, and work hard and efficiently, and possess good contacts. Admittedly luck does come into it: being at the right place at the right time matters. But unless you show that you have the ability, knowledge, or experience, then simply being there is unlikely to be enough. You must be ready to grasp the opportunity when it appears. Remember! This opportunity probably does not appear to you and to you alone. Others are likely to be waiting to seize it also.

The good news is that you can strengthen your willpower. Once you set yourself a task, especially one that you do not find all that pleasant and then you achieve it, you have made a good start. Any tasks you set yourself in the future will be slightly easier even if they do not feel so immediately. You are getting practice at succeeding and as they say, practice makes perfect. To be frank, this is not *q*uite true. Practice makes for improvement but few people or things are totally perfect.

When you achieve such a task you are actually strengthening your willpower in the same way that an exercised muscle builds up over time. Persistence.... stubbornness.... determination; such words describe attributes that can help you in this self-improvement goal. Not quitting is itself a virtue.

What other reasons are there for increasing your motivation?

A strong motivation is desirable for reasons other than simply overcoming the bad habit of putting things off.

Motivated people generally seem happier. They have a purpose in their existence, life beckons them, and they respond eagerly. They are not bored. They do not have to wonder what they want to do or how to pass the time. Probably they find the day too short to do all the things that interest them and time does not weigh heavily on their hands.

Happy people tend to get sick less than miserable ones. Whether this is due to psychosomatic or physical reasons is uncertain. Maybe the immune system takes a bit of a breather when one is bored and listless. It is clear that there is a strong link between mind and body. The body reacts to mental stimulus even if this is involuntary. Should you feel terribly afraid you might start to tremble; a suggestive or other remark might cause you to blush; an unpleasant thought can lead you to involuntarily sighing, and so on. The mind clearly has effects on the body but we are unsure of the exact mechanisms.

Because motivated people are happy and happy people get sick less often then it is hardly surprising that, on average, motivated people live longer. What might be surprising is that those who undertake voluntary work tend to live longer too, as well as being generally healthier. Some wag once remarked that volunteering is so good for you that you'd think they would make it compulsory. If you happen to be retired, or semi-retired, and do not wish to die in the near future then undertaking voluntary work is worth a thought. If you are young and still in education undertaking some voluntary work might not only improve your health but it also looks good on your CV and can help you get a job. A cynical view? Maybe. But you will also benefit personally by learning more about the world you live in, meeting new and perhaps very different people, and learning from them or perhaps learning how to cope with them. You may also develop new and fascinating interests. It might even turn out to be the start of your career. It will certainly assist you in the process of growing up.

Motivated people tend to have more friends: if one is happy, outgoing, a live-wire, and interested and involved in many things, one is more attractive to others.

Miserable people on the whole repel. A few human beings are loners, hermits, or recluses but most of us are social animals and tend to be gregarious. Even if one is something of a loner, a set of friends and a supportive network are desirable for basic survival as well as for a generally better and happier life.

Most people would prefer the world in general and their friends in particular not to see and describe them in ways such as: "Miserable old codger" (you can fill in any stronger word you like here). Such a description is not one that I think most of us would enjoy hearing about ourselves.

The key to motivation is often simply being interested in the topic or task. You probably have some hobby, sport or past-time that you enjoy. You will happily do it, watch it, read about it, and talk about it, quite possibly for hours. While doing so it does not seem tedious or boring to you. You are interested so you are motivated.

Compare that with being told to write an essay on something you feel is boring, or having to do some household chore such as vacuuming the carpets. You are unlikely to find this interesting; you probably do not want to do it; and you do not feel the need to talk about the details of it with your friends. Motivation, where art thou?

Motivation varies a lot between individuals

Why are some people more motivated than others? It is the result of a mixture of nature and nurture, which is to say what you were initially born with and then what happened to you along the line. There is nothing you can do about the first and not much about the second. But there are still plenty of things that you can do to strengthen your motivation.

A teacher telling you to buckle down and work harder or parents trying to bully you into spending more time doing homework and studying might be effective for you. On the other hand it might put your back up and instil feelings of rebellion, which are common enough anyway as teenagers naturally grow up and slide away from the iron grip of parents. If this sounds like you then telling you to buckle down is probably counter-productive. In your case, the wagging finger or shaking fist of either teachers or parents is not very likely to force you to develop self-motivation. Fear is not the key here. If you really want to do something you are likely to concentrate more and work at it both more enthusiastically and for longer. Think back to that sport, hobby or interest you already have - it is probable that you work at it hard. Why? Because your self-motivation is strong.

It is possible that you have few if any hobbies or interests in the real world. You might restrict much of your involvement to the digital area, perhaps sitting in your bedroom, communicating by phone, and participating in the online community. If you tend to spend a lot of time on the internet, chatting in social groups and the like, you might well have filled your life with ready-made entertainment. This comes to you, rather than you going out to create a real active involved life. Sooner or later you will discover that life is better if you go and embrace it and actively participate in it: it is better to be a doer than a watcher.

Cultures and nations vary *q*uite a lot and you are a member of yours. In some societies, hard work and striving are considered the norm and those who are less enthusiastic about making the effort are seen as a little strange or even downright peculiar. In other societies just getting by might be acceptable and those striving hard to improve and succeed might be looked down on, or even regarded as "tall poppies" and it is alright or even desirable to cut them down. Many think that the Chinese and Japanese have a culture that encourages striving and places a high value on education. As I have no wish to offend I shall deliberately refrain from naming possible countries, cultures, or sub-groups within a nation that might be more laid back and less inclined to encourage their children to effort but they do exist and I have lived in some of them.

Families also vary. If you come from a family that owns a lot of books and supported and encouraged you as a child to do well at school, to do your homework, to pass exams and pass them well, then you are more likely to be motivated. You accept their values, even if you rail at them sometimes, and as a result you are more likely to succeed in life. I assume here that "to succeed" means getting a good job that is enjoyable, pays well, and offers you scope for advancement. If your idea of success is to be a beachcomber on a tropical island then the advice here is not for you but then you are probably not reading this book in any case. Middle class families in general tend to push their children to succeed, in some cases perhaps too much where they overestimate the ability and potential of their offspring. We hear about "Tiger Mothers", those who constantly push their children, organize a fulltime schedule of out of school work or special classes, employ private tutors and so forth. Many of the reports tend to have a critical slant to them.

It is common for immigrant families to succeed relative to the native-born population. This is generally down to a mixture of natural selection, for those who move to a new country tend to be above average ("Those with the get up and go got up and went"), plus a lessened or maybe absent compulsion to strictly obey the mores and values of the new society they live in. Migrants, many of whom might feel that they do not totally fit in, mostly work harder and in many cases longer and better than the native- born. This accounts in large part for the success of the Overseas Chinese, the Overseas Indians, and the Jews. Many migrants often feel a strong need to ensure that their children should do well in the new country in both financial and career terms and strongly encourage them to study and work hard. Tiger Mothers are often found in migrant groups.

If you come from one of the more natural "encourage the children to work hard" groups you probably do not need extra motivation. You're lucky! You've got it already! If you come from an unsupportive background then you could certainly use help to develop your full potential. Learning the hard way certainly teaches you lessons but although experience is a good teacher it certainly exacts a high price.

Procrastination can be a problem. Many people have

difficulty getting down to a task that they know they must do but really do not feel like doing. It is never difficult to think of something else that one would find preferable, even if that is just sitting daydreaming. If this describes you, don't worry about it. This is perfectly normal and it means that you are definitely a human being and not a robot manufactured in some factory neither are you an alien dropped in from outer space.

Procrastinating can be a particular problem for many in their teen years. You are growing up, gradually ceasing to be a child and moving towards adulthood. Your body starts to alter and is not just growing larger it is changing. Your hormones kick in and the mind tends to engage in new and definitely fascinating daydreams that involve potential sexual partners. This seductively attractive new world beckons strongly. Schoolwork and college work may not hold as much attraction now as they once did. Well, that's what growing up involves. You have to learn how to strike a balance between two things: first, the new and delightful longings and urges that infest you, even if they might puzzle you a bit; and, second, growing up and becoming more mature before you embark on the journey of adult life.

Giving in totally to the seductive longings is likely to lead to you starting a family early, settling down when young, and losing out on a lot of enjoyable and valuable experiences, at least if you are unlucky. Not for nothing has the phrase "the selfish gene" been coined: in the young of any species the sexual urge is strong and the animal nature in you wants you to breed and multiply to keep the species going. I once heard teenagers described as "Walking hormonal time bombs".

Blindly following the alternative path of developing a career to the exclusion of personal friendships can lead to later regrets when you see people you know enjoying their family situation and you start to consider the possibility of a lonely middle-age or a solitary old-age.

Given these powerful forces acting upon you and the need to establish a balance between them it is hardly surprising that your motivation to work can suffer. Indeed it would be remarkable if such forces did not have an effect on you.

Your peer group also brings pressure to bear. If you are surrounded by hard working strongly motivated people then it is easier for you to work. Private schools are more often like this and of course they often have great surroundings, first-class equipment, and excellent teachers. So do some state schools; but too many such schools have a few pupils who really do not wish to learn and do not really want to be there at all. They tend to behave destructively, disrupt classes, and might as a group band up against and bully those who wish to try hard and study. They can make life a misery for the brainier and more achieving ones, with sneers and jibes such as geeks, nerds, swots, or teacher's pet. They might indulge in physical punishments and torment, or pursue cyber-bullying of a chosen individual on social network sites. It can be tough for the victim to try to do well under such circumstances. Very sadly, we read occasional reports of some poor victims choosing suicide as a way out.

If the list of things you can do to help motivate yourself seems daunting, do not worry. You do not have to do them all, or even most of them. You might find some of them appeal to you more than others. So if you choose to adopt just a few of them, fine. On the whole the more you try the more you will help yourself, but don't be afraid to start just because there seem to be a lot of suggestions. That is all they are: suggestions.

You will probably find some improvement appears quite quickly but it is best not to expect an instant dramatic leap. It is likely to take some time for you to reform an ingrained habit but any improvement will be permanent, so stay with it!

The main ways you can work on your motivation

1. Developing a good personal and psychological mind set.
2. Putting up wall posters and other visual reminders.
3. Sharing the burden and making it a game.
4. Other things that you can do.

How are you spending your time? A good way to start is to try to cultivate the attitude that the job you start must be finished - you can take breaks but your efforts should continue until the whole job is done. This might take a few hours or even days but that does not matter. Focusing on tackling and finishing tasks is a real benefit for you because you are developing your ability to concentrate and improving your self- discipline. If you learn it is OK to quit then it can become a bad habit. Not good!

When I worked in a factory as a student, it was drilled into me as a mantra that "The job isn't over until you've tided up afterwards!" I have never forgotten these words of advice. They help to stop me from giving up so that I am able to finish the undertaking at hand.

If you are not keen on doing a task, keep reminding yourself that the sooner you start, the sooner you will finish. This is true of both studying and tackling any job you should be doing but are loathe to begin. Once you start doing the job you are likely to develop some interest in it, which can help you to continue. While working at it you can congratulate yourself that you have already completed some of the task, eventually even a lot, and much of it is now behind you.

If you get a feeling of distaste when you think of a task that you know you have to do but do not feel like, stop and consider why you have to do it, what benefits might flow from tackling it, and what might go wrong for you if you do not do it. Finally you might start to think about what the task itself is about. Hey! You have just begun.

Smart phones and the like with easy access to social media can be a major distraction and eat into your available time. It is not always a treat to tweet. Turn them off! It's time to open your class or lecture notes or text book and do some real work. Keep your computer for investigating the job in hand and ignore emails and the social networking sites.

Read the material in the book, the notes, or online carefully but not in a bored and resentful way. Try to think about what you are reading. What is the main message? Is it new to you? How does the information fit in with what you already know or believe? What are the implications for other areas of interest? Do you recall the names of any author, politician or other authority figure who supports this view? Or any that oppose it? Reading and at the same time thinking about the content develops you and helps you to remember more of what you read as well as building up your interest. Yup, that's motivation!

If the mere idea of turning off your phone seems too painful even to contemplate, you can try using it as a reward: "I shall study for one full hour, and then turn it on again for ten minutes. After that, I'll do the whole process again!" If you have a habit of spending hours watching TV, especially day-time programs, you might try it for that too.

The two main approaches to improvement: "carrots" and "sticks"

Well, that's set the scene for working on your motivation. Now let's think about how you can improve it. Starting with the personal and psychological elements there are two main approaches that you can improve your motivation: carrots and sticks. The imagery comes from an analogy with driving a donkey. One can either hang a carrot in front of it and it so willingly moves forward as it likes the reward of eating; or one can hit it with a stick and it moves forward, if unwillingly, because it does not like the pain that comes from standing still. Since you are trying to improve your own motivation you can use both carrots and sticks on yourself. You are not likely to use the stick method enough to torture yourself, just to give yourself a *q*uiet poke to encourage improvement. If you should feel the temptation to cause yourself real pain it is better not to give in to it.

You are your own individual and individuals vary a lot. Some carrots and sticks will work better than others for person A, but a different set of carrots and sticks might work better for person B. I cannot tell which ways will suit you best and in advance neither can you. I suggest you try them all out, decide which you like and seem to work well in your case and stick to those. If trying them all seems too much to ask, then simply have a go at as many as you feel like.

May I stress that reading about ways of improving yourself is only a beginning if a good one: but it is the doing that will count. When you put this book down, try out one of the suggestions, any one. This will be your beginning, your wake-up call, your epiphany.

A. "The carrots" as part of your mind set

Your are likely to prefer rewards to punishments, whether self-administered or not, so I shall start with the various ways you can reward yourself in order to encourage you to get down to it. The sort of things that appeal to you could be almost anything. You might want riches, power, a better and more interesting job than you currently have, to travel and see the world, to work abroad, to own your own business, or simply to enjoy yourself.

List while I woo thee: make a list

Start by considering what you want out of life. Maybe this will be a well-paid job, or you would like to be President or Prime Minister, to live in a villa in France....

whatever. Spend some time on this and write down everything that sounds attractive to you. This list is important and if you keep it you can use it later as a strong motivator. Number your desires if you like; renumber them when you want; add to it over time; and alter it in any way you wish. You might like to call this list "Life Goals" or something like that. Hide it away if you fear that your family or friends might read it and scoff. You want no negative associations attached to it. It is really an extension of you, a groping towards your own future as a human being. Do make it your own personal list and not just things your parents or friends talk about; after all it's your life.

Dig this list out every day and read over it. Don't just skim it but read it carefully and spend a few seconds considering each point. This helps develop your motivation as your goals strengthen in your mind.

A second and more specific list might also be useful to you . Whatever your first and strongest goal is, be it to get to university, to become a doctor, to enter politics and end up as a Minister or anything else, this second list matters too. You can call it something like "Why I want to be a Minister and what must I do to achieve this".

Then fill out your reasons for wanting it and what steps might be needed to achieve it.

You can also read this list on a daily basis for the constant reminder can help build up your desire to succeed.

If you have no particular special job etc., in mind, forget the specific list and do not worry. In my teens I had no idea of what I wanted to do either. Only when I went to university in my twenties after a strange series of jobs (shop assistant, rent collector, farm labourer, soldier, musician) did I realize what I wanted to do. In my case this

was to become a university lecturer. I made it: in fact I did rather better and became a senior-lecturer, then turned down a professorship. Eventually you will discover what you want to do.

Would a job be an invasion of your privacy?

Probably not! It is the path to new and better things. So think about that great new job you will get as a result of your efforts. Studying now, or working hard at what you are doing, is likely to develop your talents or widen your contacts. Either will enable you to do work that is really interesting and will earn you good money. There might possibly be other perks that come with this good job, such as buying things more cheaply, lower-cost travel, or good working conditions, not to mention the chance to build up even better connections for your future.

Consider how much you will enjoy being the Head of Department, the surgeon, or whatever hoped for job you came up with on your earlier list. You will enjoy the work, the days will be fun not boring, the financial rewards will be good, you will avoid suffering years of *q*uiet desperation; life in fact is going to be beautiful.

Families are like fudge - mostly sweet but with a few nuts

Contemplate how happy your family will feel when you succeed. They will! They will be proud of you and your successes and this will give them something to tell to scattered family members or boast about at work. Your friends should feel happy for you too. If they do not do this but indicate that they resent your success, they are not really your friends anyway. Better dump them and find ones who are more supportive.

CHAPTER 9: SELF-IMPROVEMENT, SELF-HYPNOSIS

Also called auto-suggestion this was first recommended by the Frenchman Émile Coué and it seems to work for a lot of people. Coué also came up with the concept of "the placebo effect", which is generally accepted in medical circles, that if a person believes strongly that a harmless substance will cure him or her, then their health does actually improve. Some allege that homeopathy might work like this but I hasten to add that I have no views on the matter. A definite "Maybe" is the best that I can come up with. Coué was himself a pharmacist and knew of what he spoke.

Auto-suggestion requires you to do something. Each day, or better yet several times a day, you repeat a phrase or mantra, either out loud or in your head. This persuades your sub-conscious mind to accept it and you gradually improve. You might find that your sub-conscious often resists for a few days as it worries about this new process and is trying to keep you safe. Once it accepts that it is harmless, and then useful, it takes it on board and you start to improve. Many people use it in order to relax and as a form of meditation (e.g., "I am calm, relaxed and feeling sleepy.") I personally do this after I have gone to bed and it helps me to fall asleep. By the way, "meditation" is not a freaky thing done only by bearded weirdoes in mountain caves; many successful businesspeople and politicians do it regularly. Nor is it a religious or spiritual thing. Meditation can go with both of these but neither are essential to it or even a part of it. It is just a way of calming your mind and relaxing your body. There are strong health benefits from doing both.

Here we are interested in using auto-suggestion to boost your enthusiasm, motivation, and self-regard. With this in mind you might choose the classic mantra "Every day in every way I'm getting better and better". Or it might help if you could develop something more structured to your needs, e.g., "I feel confident, I enjoy reading history, and will do well in the exam"; or "I am a good person and improving each day"; or "I am in charge of my own life and I am happy and confident "). You can work out any phrase you like, whatever seems appropriate to you and suits your needs. It is worth spending a few minutes considering various alternatives and selecting the one that seems to fit you best.

Even a really short one, such as "Yes I can!" has power; President Obama once used the phrase "Yes we can!" as an election slogan and it seemed to help his cause. It's down to you to think up something relevant and powerful. It is best not to make it too long; and for some reason a few linked phrases seem to work best for me ("Because I feel A, B and C I am D, E and F". These are all positive good things. Choose carefully what to substitute for yourself.) When you have decided on what the main problems are that you wish to tackle, and hit on a good form of words to do this, it is a good idea to write them down and keep the piece of paper. If in doubt later, particularly in the early days, check it. The words you think or say should be identical each time and you should not paraphrase.

If your circumstances and needs change, as will likely be the case, you can change your personal mantra.

If you respond to strong visual imagery you might find "seeing" the phrase in your mind helps, and putting it into colour, such as blazing red or bright yellow works best for you.

If you are finding it difficult to raise any enthusiasm about an assignment or similar, you might find mentally repeating the phrase "I want to do this; I want to do this now" helps you settle down to the task. Repeat it a few times as you are gathering any material you need, organizing your desk, finding your pen and the like. Note: it is inadvisable to change the word to anything like "I have to do this"; you are trying to boost your own desire and having to do something suggests you are being forced to do it and you are subconsciously likely to resent this so it will probably not help you.

May your God be with you

If you have a religious belief, why not make full use of it? You can pray to your God or Gods, Saints, Bodhisattva or Spirits and ask for their assistance. Getting started on a task can be the hardest part so asking for help in order to get you going is a good idea. Once you have begun you are likely to develop interest in what you are doing and of course you can ask for help with this as well. The stronger your faith, the better the results are likely to be here.

A. The sticks as part of your mind set

You need to be careful using sticks to motivate yourself. For those who lack confidence, who worry about their abilities, who feel that they may not be up to the task, who generally tend to be of a nervous disposition or feel worthless, using sticks is sometimes unhelpful and can even be dangerously counter-productive. For such people the use of sticks can reinforce their negative attitudes and make them even less keen to start a task. This is of course the exact opposite of what is needed.

Even worse, the use of sticks could damage them as human beings as they might lead to suffering and distress or even perhaps to more serious mental problems. Clinical depression is an awful thing and anything that could induce it should be avoided. If you feel you might be in or near this category you would be wise to choose carrots and stick to using them. If you are unfortunate enough ever to have indulged in self-harm then in your case sticks are probably best avoided.

In contrast to this, for those who brim with self-confidence, who never question themselves or their decisions, and assume that they are always or mostly right sticks are likely to be far less of a danger. I have noticed that some people do not listen to the arguments of others but only look as if they are doing so and are really just waiting for the chance to get in and make their own points. They are often secretly rehearsing these in their mind as they appear to be listening. A little stick would probably do t hem no harm.

Assuming that you feel that sticks might be for you, here goes.

If you sit still long enough you might get a dead-end

Spare a thought for what awaits those without **q**ualifications - dead-end jobs are a likely outcome. These are usually boring and generally underpaid. If you become caught in this way it can be very depressing. Actually, an even worse future for those who drop out early might be no job at all because we live in a world where skills increasingly matter and simple repetitive or labouring jobs are more and more done by machines. Being unemployed is destructive to human beings because part of self- worth seems to be having a job and feeling of value in society. For some people, living on handouts from the state might seem to be not too bad but it actually can be most harmful. Many people who do this become resigned to it, start to see it as a normal way of living, begin to believe that it is their right to live off others, and in effect they cease to be responsible individuals and a part of modern society. In addition, they will never accumulate a personal pension and we know that the state pension is not enough to live on comfortably; this is the case now but in the future state pensions are likely to be even less generous as governments tighten up.

Jobs such as shelf-stacking, or standing with a board outside a shop advertising burgers, buffet lunches or boots, leads nowhere for the majority. You would not want to be doing this aged sixty-five or older either. This might seem like a long way off to you but people are living longer and eventually you will probably have to face old age. You may not look forward to getting old but if you think about it, it is worse if you suddenly stop doing so.

Oh, the shame of it all!

If you are considering dropping out, spare a thought about what your family and friends will say, or, if they are kind enough to avoid criticizing you, think about you. If you drop out and demonstrate failure you can be reasonably sure that behind your

back gossip will thrive. It's not a nice feeling to keep wondering what people might be saying about you. Harness this feeling of shame to help you buckle down to work now.

I've got to get out of this place

One possible stick might be that you want to leave the town you live in and go to someplace more interesting. Should this be the case, then you can remind yourself that hard work and studying will help get you out. Onwards and upwards!

My kingdom for a horse - or other goodies

Another stick might be that you want a lot of things that you currently do not possess. Maybe these are fashionable clothes, the latest gadgets and technology items, foreign holidays, or visiting expensive clubs (which might mean better clothes too). If these all sound good to you then tell yourself that the way to get these is to work longer, harder, and better.

Burning your bridges might help

In a war, a retreating army destroys bridges behind it to make life harder for the enemy. In today's world, the modern equivalent is making a precommitment. This means making your mind up to do something then taking action that makes it more likely that you will follow through. It can take a variety of forms but all involve a modicum of self-discipline. It is not completely foolproof. Actually nothing ever is: when we think we have finally made something foolproof someone comes along and invents a better fool. An example of a precommitment is signing up for gym membership. Although statistics reveal that the dropout rate of those who sign up is high, such a precommitment might still be worth doing as the process can help us to overcome our desire for instant gratification. It can be of value in helping to tackle the undesirable habit of "fast thinking" and gain the long term benefits of "slow thinking".

2. You know where you can stick it

Wall posters, stick-it notes, and visual reminders can help generate enthusiasm for the task in hand. You can encourage yourself by putting up posters and notes around your bedroom. These serve the dual purpose of reminding you that you want to succeed and also drive the message into your subconscious that you are taking it seriously and really really mean it. You can stick these messages up anywhere you like: on the wall, on cupboard doors, hanging below pictures, on your bedhead A small card sitting in the top of a drawer that you open a lot might work for you.

What sort of message might work best? The actual content is down to you and your needs. Something like "I must get to university"; "I really want to get in to XXX college"; "I need at least three A's and a B in the exams"; "A good degree will get me into the job I want"; "Start studying, darn it!"; "I've got to get out of this town and that degree will help do it!"; "Daddy will buy me a new BMW if I pass" (well, maybe he won't). Perhaps the two lists you made earlier could go up if you find it helps.

If you observe that after a while you are starting to ignore your wall notes, try moving them around so they are not in the same place as last week. Or maybe adding a bit of new colour would help. Re-write them in red or any colour other than the one you were using previously. Or perhaps you could add a big red blob next to a phrase or two to draw the eye or maybe use highlighter to make it stand out.

Some people find that putting up a photograph or picture of whatever they would like out of life helps their motivation. It might be a sports car, a pretty house, or a motorboat that you would like to own. Or it could be a picture of the Taj Mahal if you would like to visit India and travel the world. You can add encouraging words underneath the pictures in order to increase the allure of these wonderfully attractive things.

When you feel bored, fed up, and not in the mood for studying, walking around the room looking and reading might help you get back to work. If you were studying, then got bored and stopped, try taking a short break of maybe ten to twenty minutes before you examine your posters or pictures. This might help you to go back to it.

3. Gamesmanship: winning matters - it's why they keep score

You can share the burden and turn studying into a game. It's study-buddy time! I strongly recommend that you find someone to study with. Let's be up front about this. If you are using your "Going round to X's to study" as an excuse to your parents so that you can go someplace else such as a shopping mall, or maybe you really do intend to go round to X's but to engage in .... how can I put this delicately? some

social activity that seems much more desirable than studying, this is not what I mean. You need to get together in order to work and improve your exam results not just to skive off.

Here are a few ways of working together for you to consider. They all do roughly the same thing: you consider a problem or topic, you decide what you think, then you explain it to someone else. You can ask questions and argue as you go and this is a valuable thing to do. The process itself helps to boost your interest and to lock information more firmly into your memory, and it also gives you a conversation to look back on and recall later. This might prove very useful in the exam room. The various games are just different ways of doing this.

As a bonus, if you choose you can finish up by drafting a written outline or skeleton answer that you and your study-buddy can file away. The outline is going to be short, snappy and to the point and it will make an excellent piece to use for revision later on.

Try a few of the games or try them all if you like. See which ones you prefer. Even if you only do one of them and ignore the others, it can help improve your motivation as well as your memory of things you are supposed to know and might be tested on.

If you have just been set homework or an assignment to write then you might find it useful to sit and talk about the question with your study-buddy and decide what you think about it before tackling the project in detail. Depending on your subject, the level you are at, and the question itself, your discussion might involve things such as what factors might be involved; how important each of them is; what were the causes; what were the effects; what were the intended results and were there any unintended results; or are there any important names associated with the issue that you can quote. You might also consider if there might be different ways of tackling the question and which is likely to be the best.

The preparation of your answer is usually more important to your learning than actually writing it up although this is a bit less so if you happen to be in the literary or English area. In that case the actual words you choose do matter of course and with writing, as with most things, the more you practise the better you get at it.

CHAPTER 10: THE GAMES

If you think of the preparatory stage of tackling a question as a game for two people it can seem more interesting and less of a burdensome chore. Here are a few such games that you can play that can increase your motivation and at the same time improve the *q*uality of your answers. Any notes you take can provide excellent means of revising in the future. You can invent your own game if you can think of a fun way that fits your own needs better.

Game 1 Explaining the Topic: Notes or Worksheets

Each of you takes the same short topic in a particular subject and reads over his or her own notes for maybe five or ten minutes. How long it takes depends on you, the particular discipline you are studying, and the complexity of the question. Then close your notes and each one explains the topic to the other. If you falter, you are allowed a quick look at your notes, but then close them again and continue the explanation. If you are at high school and have been given worksheets you could use a suitable one of those instead.

Ask questions, *q*uery what you hear, and talk about it. It is up to you whether you interrupt and ask *q*uestions, or jot down a *q*uestion as you listen and save them up for the end of the short talk. The latter is more common at seminars at the university level and getting in the habit now would do you no harm. Once you are involved in discussing the issue you can use your notes, refer to books, or use whatever helps your argument or the point that you are making. The discussion can expose weak points in your knowledge and help you fill them. Comes the exam, if a question comes up that is relevant there is a good chance that you will remember the conversation and have little trouble answering the pesky *q*uestion. It may even improve the logical way you argue and develop your ability to persuade another to your point of view. All good stuff!

Note that trying to teach someone is a very good way of learning it for oneself. First, it really can boost your motivation as you grapple with the issues, try to understand them, then explain the whole thing in a simple way. It also digs the information deeper into your memory. So the more you do this kind of thing, the better you get. It is much more effective than just sitting reading notes and trying not to let your mind wander. It is really likely to want to do this especially if you have a short attention span.

Game 2 Tackling Old Exam Questions

Take any old exam question and talk with your study-buddy about possible ways of tackling it; there may be several, some better than others. Then it's time to think about what particular points might go into the answer. A quick recheck: after you have noted down a few points do any of them affect the choice of the best way to tackle the question? Then taking, say, five minutes you each individually prepare an outline answer to this question (no talking now!). Start with the main body of the answer, listing the points you can think of, then maybe numbering them in what seems to you to be a sensible order.

You can then compare your skeleton outlines, see any differences, decide what points should go in, and in what best logical order. It is wise to put the most important points upfront because markers expect to see this and it suggests to them that you are good and if they develop a favourable attitude towards you it can help you get better marks. Finally, you can talk about what would be a good introduction and conclusion. A wise person once said that when answering a question you say everything three times: the Introduction indicates briefly what you are about to say; the middle bit gives the answer; and the Conclusion briefly sums up what you just said. Do make sure that the Introduction and Conclusion line up and do not contradict in any way!

If you both prefer, rather than be together to work out your individual answers you could each think about the answer and draw up an outline before you meet. A benefit of this is that you can compare both outlines immediately then discuss a good approach to the question and desirable points to include and in what order. Finally you can combine your skeleton outlines to get the best possible answer. Whichever way seems good to you probably will be.

Keep going until you feel that you have done enough, then take a break.

A variation, that might work better after you have a little experience of doing the same question, would be to take different exam *q*uestions each and explain them to the other.

Game 3 Explaining a Different Topic to Each Other

In advance you both agree on the same general subject and then you each select a different topic within that area. In this way you both know what topic the other person will cover and have geared yourself up to the general area. Then each of you explains as much as he or she can remember to the other but without reference to notes. Then the explainer opens his or her notes and goes through, seeing what was missed and explaining that part too. You can then talk about it together. The listener may want to ask *q*uestions, criticize and argue. This is good and should be done wherever possible as it makes you defend your position and really get a feel for the topic.

When one has finished, if you are both exhausted, take a break. Otherwise the other person starts with his or her different topic and repeats the process. If you did not break in the middle, consider taking a good break after the second person has finished in order to clear your heads for Round Two.

Game 4 Swapping Subject Information

If you are good at, say, history and your buddy is good at geography, you can each take one topic from your favourite discipline and explain it to the other. You might point out what use it is in the world, why it is important to know, how it relates to other theories, issues or parts of the world, in addition to explaining the issue itself. It is a good idea to set a time limit for each person, maybe ten minutes or whatever works best for you both. Then comes question and discussion time. After that you could take a break, switch roles, and move to the other discipline

Game 5 Flash Card Time

If you have already made flash cards that summarise information that you need to learn you can hand your cards to your study-buddy and get him or her to test you, card by card. Naturally you can only do this if you have already spent time going over your flash cards and studying them. Swap the roles of *q*uestioner and answerer whenever you like.

You can also make use of your buddy's flash cards in the same way. You might spend a few minutes studying their card or cards first then hand them back and get them to test you. Using someone else's flash cards like this can help to give you a different and broader perspective on an issue.

A cautionary if repetitive note: if your study-buddy is of the opposite sex, or you simply fancy them rotten, make sure you really are studying and not socializing in some way! Best save your smooching session or whatever for non-study periods.

4. Other Things That You Can Do

a) Organize a good place for you to work and get the environment right. In this case, "right" means whatever helps you to concentrate and settle down to the job in hand. The room you choose can be important. Some people, I for one, like working in a library and I often choose that to study in; others like their bedroom, or maybe the kitchen. If you have not thought about this before, try a few different places and see which is the most conducive to studying for you.

b) If you are studying in your own place and not in a library, you might find that playing background music helps you to concentrate - me, I found this distracting and I prefer to listen to music solely for enjoyment and to relax. Though if you are in a library I guess you could always use high quality earphones to avoid annoying other users and the gorgon-like librarians (well, at least where I live). I find earphones with a noise-cancelling facility the best to use but they are not cheap. Recent research into listening to music while studying suggests that music really is a distraction and it reduces your learning ability even if you think it helps. Those who listened to music scored noticeably less on testing than those who studied in silence. What listening to music while studying may do is make you feel better about the whole process. If this leads you to study more often and for a longer time, it might pay off in total. However, a shorter period of silent study might be a more efficient way of achieving the same results! You have to make a choice here....

If you are at work and trying to concentrate on a project there is usually little that can be done about your surroundings. You might be able to brighten it up and make it feel a little more like somewhere you would choose to be. A photograph of your family or pet, a pot plant, some weird souvenir you bought on vacation, stuff like that. Perhaps a motivational quote propped up where you can see it which you can easily change, perhaps on a daily basis, might help you. There are heaps of such self- improvement mottos that you can download freely from the Internet and print up for yourself.

c) Good lighting and a decent temperature help because anything that could possibly distract you needs avoiding. Above all, loud extraneous noises can be most off-putting. I was trying to write a small section of this book when builders suddenly started work next door, using pneumatic drills or jack hammers depending which culture you come from. In the end I simply had to give up the attempt to think and write. Luckily for me they finished the noisy digging out part of their work in a few hours. Universities seem to be under constant rebuilding or extending, at least those I have worked in. They can be noisy places.

As a student there is nothing you can do. If you are already working for a living a word to your boss might lead to some improvements; maybe double-glazing or noise insulation boards could be installed for example. If you point out that it would be good for the firm's profit levels if people were less distracted it might strengthen your case. Higher profit is generally a good argument.

d) If you use a tablet or laptop for studying, whether writing, or revising, and find it hard to resist the lure of the time-draining social networks then maybe you should choose to work in a Wi-Fi-free zone. If you are unable get out onto the internet then you might be able to focus better on what you really should be doing.

e) The above words look at where to study or work. Consider also your best time of the day to study. Everyone seems to have a diurnal cycle, where they feel listless or sleepy for an hour or so in the day, and yet at other times their energy level is higher. I personally am in a mental low spot between about 4 pm and 6 pm and therefore I structure my day to take account of this.

Sometimes such a recurrent down period can be the

result of low blood sugar. If you suspect this might be the case, try eating a piece of fruit. It is not just healthy in general but the complex carbohydrates break down more slowly than a sugary drink. Incidentally, so-called healthy fruit juice drinks are not all that healthy because often sugar has been added, sometimes a lot. This means that fresh fruit is always a healthier option to juice.

f) How long should you study without a break? Individuals vary but a period of around an hour to an hour and a quarter is often about right. After that, the level of concentration tends to slump quite dramatically and although you are putting the time in, the quality of what you are doing will probably suffer. Four straight hours of studying is likely to produce poorer results for you than two sessions of an hour and a quarter with a thirty minute break between. If you try a few sessions of forty-five minutes then a short break; then increase it to an hour then a break; then an hour and a quarter with a break you could see which suits you best. If you come the conclusion that you are a ten minute guy then this clearly is too short. Work on your motivation! g) If you are studying at home and face a long period of study, you might find that a short mid-afternoon nap between sessions helps you. "Short" might mean half an hour or a bit less, not the rest of the day in bed. The occasional catnap is often beneficial for the quality of your work. Some of history's great achievers did this: Napoleon, Leonardo da Vinci, Thomas Edison, Eleanor Roosevelt, and Winston Churchill were just some of them. It has been discovered that a short nap of twenty minutes up to about forty-five minutes improves concentration, memory recall and general health.

h) Giving yourself a small treat as a reward for achieving a goal you set can be a big help in improving motivation. Maybe you would enjoy a coffee once you have studied for one hour, or carefully planned out an answer and given it a lot of thought. That was the kind of lure that for many years kept me at the soul-destroying task of marking exam papers "Six more scripts and I'll drink that coffee and eat a small piece of dark chocolate!"

i) If you have to tackle something you dislike doing, you might choose the morning as the best time rather than attempting it later in the day. People tend to have more energy in the mornings after a good night's sleep and that should help get on with this loathsome task. The actual process of considering the various jobs you need to do, determining which one you will do first, then settling down to it and finishing can help you too. It can toughen up your attitude, strengthen your self-discipline, and develop your ability to get stuck in when you need to. When you have actually completed the task it can also give you a sense of achievement and this can increase your general sense of self-worth. It's a win-win situation!

j) As a student you need to keep track of your classes. If you make a weekly timetable of your school classes and carry it around with you, then it might help increase your motivation if you dig it out at quiet moments, such as waiting at the bus stop, and look it over. Try to think positively about it; maybe say mentally something like, "Hey, these look good!", "I'm working my way to a great future!", or something that you will find encouraging. This is particularly useful if you are already at college or university with their various lectures, tutorials, lab sessions, and the like. This list is in addition to your daily "to-do" list.

As a worker you need to keep track of your appointments and meetings as well as things that you need to do during the day. If you are important enough to have a good PA (lucky you!) then you have fewer worries. For most of us, a list of what needs doing when helps us to survive.

k) Make sure you get enough sleep. For many in their teens this might sound like a joke: sleeping is not usually the problem. Actually, in my case not wanting to go to bed until very late and then not wanting to get out of bed the next morning was the problem. You might be the same. As an adult a challenge for me was getting some of my teenage nephews out of bed before noon. The difficulty is that teen energy levels can keep one going until four in the morning, or even all night, then one crashes out. Such behaviour might work during holidays but during term time it can become a problem. If you are tired you will not study well. Sleep deprivation has a really bad effect on the mind and the ability to concentrate or even the wish to concentrate. Sleep deprivation is a well-known torture technique to break down mental resistance.

l) Alcohol in excess can come with similar problems attached. It sure can be great fun putting it away in the company of friends and having a fantastic time. The down-side comes later. Although a little alcohol might help a person to relax and sleep better, many people drink far more than a little with the result that their sleep is broken as they stagger off to the bathroom for one reason or another (I don't do sordid details). They are then likely to sleep later and wake up with a headache and a mouth that feels like the bottom of a parrot's cage. OK, I confess that I am writing this from personal experience of my own student days. But naturally I never did this to excess. Well not much anyway. Headaches and the associated yucky feeling do not help motivation or success at anything really.

m) Eating properly is also a good idea. For many people this means a combination of eating fewer chips; eating less pre-prepared food from a supermarket that really comes from a factory (and one that you probably would not like to walk around as they can be quite unpleasant or even disgusting); and eating more fruit and vegetables. I am not a dietician but a healthy diet is conducive to being able to do better at just about anything.

n) In similar vein, you should take some regular exercise. Sport is good and the training that helps you get better at it is valuable. If like me you are not naturally good at anything just choose the one you find the least unattractive. Some sports use more muscles than others. Swimming is particularly good for all round exercise. Squash is good for aerobic exercise as it requires sudden very rapid movements followed by a slight pause and this puts stress onto the system rapidly raising the heart rate. Because of this, if your family has a history of heart attacks or stroke problems this sport might be on the dangerous side for you. In this case it is definitely worth getting a medical check up before hitting the court.

o) Another good idea is to try not to get into, and especially out of, emotional crises. Yes, a love affair can be most distracting and prevent you from studying, especially if the end of the affair is forced on you, in other words if you are dumped. There might be the occasional side benefit of this, for at one party I was at I once overheard the following.

Young woman: "I think it's time for me to start a love affair!" Her female friend: "Why for heaven's sake?"

Young woman: "Because when I end it in a few week's time it will take my appetite away and I desperately need to lose weight."

Hmm. Note that I definitely do not advocate this form of weight control program for several reasons, none of which is worth pursuing here. Just remember that emotional stress and strain are very draining and will certainly not improve your motivation to study.

When at university you will find that you have a lot of free time in which you have no lectures, etc. Don't fall into the trap of idling away your day but tackle this seductive freedom directly, using any of these tips that help you. The union bar might be a good place to relax, but it is a bad place to spend all your time! Working in the library will serve you better. And day-time television is not the best way of preparing for exams or life in general.

p) Consider your friends and the people you hang with: think about them objectively. If you believe that they put you down in some way, and perhaps treat you in a negative fashion, or that in general they despise learning and hard work, they are probably not the friends you need. They are an anchor holding you back. See if you can branch out and find more supportive friends, ones who can help you feel good about yourself and encourage you to work hard. Even one such friend is worth a lot more than a bunch of no-hopers who are influencing you to follow their example. If you are trapped in such a negative group, try to ease away from them and find and develop a new set of friends. Joining a club or society is often a good way of doing this.

q) A daily timetable is useful and gets you to the right place at the right time. Your classes and lectures should go on first then around them you can also fit in other unscheduled things that you should do, like " 3pm library: look up the theory of X" or "7pm: revise physics".

Hint: if the first point on the list is "Make list" you can cross it off *q*uickly and feel good about it! Keep on crossing off items as you finish them as this helps drive home the fact that you have accomplished something and are getting somewhere. Success tends to feed upon itself.

It can be a good idea to asterisk a couple of list items that you feel you must do rather than you simply want to do. This attracts the eye and might make you focus more on those.

Anything left undone on the list can be transferred to the next day's list. If you do this, remember to reconsider the priorities for this next day and do not automatically continue where you left off yesterday. Maybe the reason that you did not do it back then was that it was low priority but it might now have increased in urgency. Now and then you might find that something on the list that did not get done has been eclipsed by time and can be dropped from the new list: "Watch the special TV program at 8" for instance is defunct if you missed it, unless technology allows a catch-up. While you are making lists, or deciding what to do in general, keep in mind that "important" is not the same as "urgent"; remember that you need to do the urgent ones first even if something else is important and in the long term matters a lot.

r) When you have an assignment to write, or a particular report to prepare, you can set a reminder a few days before you really need to begin. Write it in your diary or else stick into your reminders/calendar on your phone, tablet, computer or whatever electronic gadget you normally use. When you reach the reminder, the jog to the memory can help you to realize its importance and put it more in the front of your mind. Whenever it starts to seem more important to you then it is. You might choose to use high-lighter pens to indicate the degree of importance or use block capitals, italics, a number of stars system or some other method. Whatever works for you is good for you.

s) Watch out for displacement activity and fight it. This is where you put off doing something that you know needs doing in order to do something else. The mind is particularly good at inventing such activity and making it feel attractive. It might suggest things like watching TV, playing cards or computer solitaire, ringing up friends to chat for hours, constantly checking on emails, making coffee, or even mundane stuff like cleaning the house. Don't fall for it!

A slightly more academic form of this, but e*q*ually dangerous, is to keep putting off writing the assignment, thesis, or report as you feel you need to do more research, read more books, talk to more friends about it and the like. All you really need to write is a computer; or, if you still do it the old-fashioned way, a pen and paper.

t) Although it is common to plan out your answer, then start writing in the planned order, that is, first the introduction, followed by the main body, and finally the conclusion, you do not actually have to write it in that order. Once you have a good planned outline you can start writing any bit that appeals first. Maybe it seems the easiest bit to you, maybe you know more about it, maybe it is a special interest of yours or at least related to one. If that bit is calling you, listen to your inner voice and start with that. It can help you in at least three ways. One, you have actually begun and without a beginning there can never be an end. Two, when you have finished that section you can feel pleased at your achievement and get a feeling of success. Three, it can raise your interest in the rest of the topic and encourage you to do more. When writing on a computer you can move stuff around anyway you like whenever you like. Just keep a few backups. I find numbering successive drafts like "Iron ore 1", "Iron ore 2", "iron ore 3" and so on very useful. When I stuff up the one I am working on, I can easily go back to the most recent version.

u) If you are working at home, leaving out the materials you are working on so that they are easily visible can help motivate you. When you see the pile of books, the heap of notes, the jotted down ideas and the like it can help increase your resolve to pick up where you left off and get on with it again. It is also *q*uicker and easier just to pick up where you left off than if you have to dig out a lot of things and organize them before you can begin. When I was learning the clarinet I discovered that leaving it out on its stand encouraged me to pick it up and practise; if I dismantled it, cleaned it and put it back in the case I did not practise anywhere near as much. It seems that I could not be bothered to make that extra little effort to take it out of the case and put it back together again. Laziness is not its own reward.

v) Relax! Sometimes you may need to slacken off to feel motivation. It is normal for people to feel tense and worried as exams approach, or a serious work deadline is approaching. Athletes often feel this before the start of a race or actors just before going on stage. If you are a person who normally worries a lot and feels tense and uptight about studying or life in general then you would almost certainly benefit from learning to relax. This may not come easily and you really have to learn how to do it and practise too.

If your are really tense you may need to take a break for a day or two and you should get away completely if you can. A total change of environment can work wonders for some. In Northern Europe and elsewhere, the winter blues can be bad. SAD, or season affective disorder, does exist. Maybe you need to chase the sun for a long weekend if you can afford it. If you can't afford it, which as a student is probable, well the good degree you will shortly get means that you soon will be able to afford it. A day's outing with a cheap coach ticket might be enough to help you relax for the present.

w) Motivation when tackling an assignment. When you have an assignment to prepare, do not keep putting it off, or sit and worry about it. A good way to start is begin with some small and simple step, such as grabbing a piece of paper and making a plan of what you will do first. Maybe "Read lecture notes on the topic and jot down any ideas I get"; "Look up the set text book"; "Find a few more text books and see what they say"; "Go to the school or Uni library and talk to the librarian about what I might read about this topic", and so forth. Just making this list can help boost your motivation.

When you have done this, make another list of whatever comes into your head about the topic itself. Perhaps this will start with some points that could go in the answer; then the name of any famous people associated with the topic, perhaps an academic, a scientist, or a politician; it might be the title of a book that you've heard of that seems relevant to the question; also you might jot down the name of someone in your school or university that you could talk to about the issue; and finally anything else at all that you can think of that might help. The process is valuable and the list you develop can be invaluable.

If you are ever faced with an assignment that seems daunting, try to tackle it by first thinking about what it might be about and what might go in; then look up your lecture notes; check the course textbook and a few other books; and finally get a pen and note down whatever you think or feel about the issue.

Go on the Internet. Wikipedia is currently a good place to start but not all the information is accurate and some people find it amusing to be deliberately misleading and feed in false information, so be careful! Nothing on the Internet is gospel truth and much of it is partial, misleading or down-right wrong. And it is better not to quote Wikipedia as a source because some academics hate to see it cited.

If someone has set a long and complicated question it might daunt you or even seem unmanageable, but a tiny piece of it should look reasonable. You might find "salami tactics" help you here. This means slicing the big task into small segments and tackling each sliver a piece at a time. Some politicians and developers adopt salami tactics to get something achieved that they fear might be resisted or rejected if it were presented as a whole, so they just keep making small decisions and nibbling away at the issue. The Chinese have a saying about tackling a huge project in this way: "Like ants gnawing away at a bone". A little reward after finishing such a draft of one tiny segment might spur you on to the next piece.

x) With a new assignment use that study-buddy

Either ring them and talk about the question or get together to work. Once you do this you are increasing your motivation. Maybe you could start by discussing the question, what factors might be involved and in what way; what the marker might expect to see included; what seem to be important points and should go in upfront or at least early on; what points seem relevant but maybe less important and so should appear later in your answer; which academics, authors, politicians, scientists and the like support the ideas (if any) and which oppose them.

You can play a few learning games, based around the assignment question or topic. This can make learning more fun and raise your level of interest in what you have to do.

Before you get together with your study-buddy you might tell them how you feel you might start, and what you intend to do next (e.g., check your class or lecture notes). Even the simple process of explaining to someone what you are about to do can help kick-start your enthusiasm. In addition, should it make you feel you had better keep your word and not look like an idiot by not doing what you said, it can help promote your motivation.

If you have not yet found a study-buddy (keep looking!) then talk to anyone around. Try a few of your friends, particularly if they have to tackle the same question; Wikipedia can help you but remember two things I said earlier: some of the information in it is quite wrong; and markers do not like to see it quoted as a source (hint, hint!). Some Internet forums can supply good advice but far too many have been taken over by spammers. If you can find a moderated one in your area of interest where someone checks all submissions before allowing them to be posted you are more likely to get good help.

y) You might also try asking a teacher or lecturer for advice. In my experience they are more likely to be sympathetic if you go in with something you have thought about and wish to discuss. They are often less sympathetic if you go in either in total ignorance and have not bothered to think about it or else you go in with a written draft and ask them to read it before submitting your final draft. Many teachers and lecturers feel it is unfair to give you two bites at the cherry but no one else gets it. They are also busy people and if word gets around that they will do this, dozens of people are likely to hammer on their door asking for their evaluation of pre- submission items.

z) If you do badly in an assignment turn this to your advantage

This is a special case of not allowing yourself to be put off by setbacks in life. Persistence is a major virtue. If you fail at something, maybe not get the job after the interview, not get your article accepted, lose the tennis or football match or whatever, do not just give up. Turn the experience to your advantage, ask yourself why you did not get the result you wanted, what you can do to change this, and take action accordingly. The next time you will be in a much stronger position to achieve your goals. Remember: the person who never made a mistake never made anything. They just existed and drifted. As the German philosopher Nietzsche once put it: "What does not kill me makes me stronger."

If a paper comes back with a poor mark, read the comments of the marker and work out why you might have done whatever they objected to; next time don't do it. Think about what you might have done in to avoid this; then next time take action. The marker might be prepared to discuss the issue with you and suggest what you might do to tackle your particular problems. It is worth asking.

Let's look at a few specifics of what might have gone wrong and what you can do about it. If your work seems generally to be of a low standard without any particular problems being isolated by the marker probably you need to work a bit harder, work more often, and work more efficiently. You just have to try to up your game.

If your problem is that you did not really answer the question that was asked then you need to concentrate on planning out your answer carefully. It helps if you keep reading the *q*uestion as you plan and later follow your prepared plan without deviation. If the comments indicated that you missed out important points then the solution involves you reading more about the problems involved; thinking more about the issues as you plan your answer; and talking more with your study-buddy. In this instance two heads are better than one at coming up with points.

If you have the problem of being too wordy and rambling (if your essay is a lot longer than anyone else's this is probably the case) then it calls for a tightening up in two areas: first at the thinking and discussing stage; and secondly during the actual writing up process. The first, or preparatory stage, gets down what you want to say (no repetition of points!). The second writing up stage is how you actually say it. The latter is probably worth a bit more attention if you are not naturally concise. Perhaps you know what you want to say but do not think long and hard about how best to say it. This is harder to tackle but you can do two things. One is to read good writers to see how they did it. I personally recommend reading and studying the sentence structure of the funny novels of P.G. Wodehouse to improve your style; and you could also try looking at the novels of Ernest Hemingway, a master of short terse sentences and economical writing. When you think you have finished the assignment you might also find it helpful to go through on a computer and edit it carefully one more time before putting the essay, report, or whatever, in. If you can wait twenty- four hours before the final edit you are more likely to notice where you can improve it.

If the problem is that your assignment could not be read because of your poor handwriting - and I can put my hand up to this one - then everything you submit should be done on the computer and printed out. I assume they still let you put in hand-written assignments but these days many teachers do not allow this. Few offices will allow it either. If you have bad handwriting you will have a problem in the exam when you will probably have to write longhand, at least with the present level of technology. I tackled my own problem here by paying for a few private handwriting lessons and buying a book of exercises to work through. Did it help? Perhaps a bit but not really a lot I confess. In my university's annual student survey of the staff, my students still complained about my handwriting. But I really did try my hardest.

Repeating an earlier suggestion, one thing you can always do is go and see the marker and ask for help and any suggestions for improvement that they might have. Well, with the exception of your lousy handwriting anyway. When they get over their initial shock it could pay off handsome dividends for you.

Take my advice and avoid assignment writers you can find on the Internet, whether they charge for their services or not. Why? You will get no personal development out of it; you are unlikely to remember much about the answer later because you put in no effort; and you are learning and rein-forcing personal bad habits that will probably harm you later and damage your life. It seems weird to me that anyone would pay good money to someone else in order to do them so much lasting harm! It might seem tempting when short of time or when looking for good marks with no effort but you'd far better not.

CONCLUSION

Many people tend to believe that procrastination is a harmless habit that cannot really create huge problems. Some people believe that finishing the task is important and it is *q*uite irrelevant when you finish it. There are artistic procrastinators who will find innovative ways to put off tasks. They know that they have about ten tasks that need their attention.

What will such procrastinating artists do? They will do the first one or two jobs and the restructure their to-do list of the remaining eight in such a way that they end up losing more time on doing unimportant things ahead of the important ones. Yes, they may complete the task but it would invariably be a sufficiently big loss of resources to themselves.

While there could be some short-term benefits of procrastination such as less stress levels earlier on, these stress levels are bound to accumulate and become one large wave threatening to consume your life if you do not find the time and energy to do all your tasks at the correct time. Procrastinators end up suffering more and performing far worse than people who do the jobs at the correct times.

The 3...2...1 trick is a wonderful way to get started on your treatment for procrastination. It has worked for me and there is no reason why it should not work for you. This trick's true potential will be felt and leveraged by you when you work just a little hard for about two weeks to make it into a habit. Only the first two weeks might seem a tad bit difficult. But, once you have crossed the 'habit threshold,' then there is nothing to stop you from achieving success in all aspects of your life!

So, 3...2...1, start off!

Lightning Source UK Ltd.
Milton Keynes UK
UKHW020658040621
384928UK00011B/729

9 781803 070940